Taken By Surprise

A Declaration of Perseverance

Taken By Surprise

A Declaration of Perseverance

KEVIN GOCKE

CONTENTS

ACKNOWLEDGMENTS

Special Thanks

I would like to extend my utmost gratitude and respect to those who have had my back, through thick and thin, both intentionally and unintentionally, throughout my journey. My family, friends, and all my loved ones may never truly understand the appreciation I have for their love and support. Writing this book has been no easy feat, as it is a culmination of my intense life experiences, and I could not have done it without my support group. My parent's unconditional love cannot be compared on any scale. They have been by my side since day one and I am forever grateful beyond words. Both my brothers stepped up to the plate during my recovery, however, they played very different roles. Bennett being the eldest truly took matters into his own hands by pulling me under his wing not only when I was at my absolute rock bottom, but also when I needed the motivation to write this book and help me throughout the process. I would also like to thank my middle brother, Spencer, for being there for me emotionally, musically and as my most trusted nail technician. The man has a gift when it comes to giving manicures. Spencer also pushed me to regain my confidence and ability to play music, despite my challenges to keep up the way I once could.

Also, I would like to express a special thanks to my wife, Kayla, who has been my loving and supportive rock in more ways than one. She has graciously put up with me scattering papers all over the office, staring off into space mid-conversation thinking about this project, and waking up in the middle of the night like a maniac to write down thoughts I refused to forget.

I am honored to have had many great teachers and mentors throughout my life who have influenced me and helped shape me into the man I am today. Some of whom I know personally and some I have yet to meet, but all have provided incredible perspective to my very unique life.

Most importantly, I would like to thank God for giving me a second chance at life. I would also like to thank all the individuals, living and nonliving, who have influenced my life as well as my recovery process. I encountered a handful of living angels in a sea of white coats when I was hospitalized. And lastly, I'd like to thank the doctors, nurses, and therapists who made my painful reality just a little bit easier for me.

A few years back, Andrew Huberman, a professor of neurobiology and ophthalmology at Stanford University School of Medicine, inadvertently became a huge mentor for my understanding of the human brain and its plasticity. He is not personally aware of his contribution to my overall success, but I owe a great sense of gratitude to him for substantiating and validating what I was naturally doing by instinct to recover, through providing peer-reviewed science, experimentation, and documentation. Andrew Huberman has also provided me with the lifestyle tools necessary to maintain these practices while discovering new and innovative ways of improving my mind and body. I can't recommend Andrew Huberman's research and findings enough.

Another noteworthy recipient of gratitude is Ed Mylett, an American businessman and motivational figure who taught me how to reframe my way of thinking in a way that leads toward action and measurable results. He has coincidentally echoed many of my preexisting philosophies and ways of living, indirectly providing me with validation that I am on the right track.

I could go on for a bit about all the inspirational figures who have motivated me, but for the sake of brevity, I will point you in the direction of these incredible individuals who have inspired me throughout my recovery in more ways than one. Here they are in no particular order:

Bill & Deborah Gocke (Mom & Dad)
Bennett Gocke (Brother)
Spencer Gocke (Brother)
Bruce Lee
Tony Robbins (Motivational Speaker)
Dr. Kenneth Lynn
Dr. Michael Aufdemberg
Tiffany (ICU Nurse)
Heather (ICU Nurse)
Bjorn Strid aka "Speed" (Soilwork Lead Vocals)
Jason Cruz (Strung Out Lead Vocals)

Dave Mathews (Musician)
Bill Burr (Comedian)
Tom Segura (Comedian)
Joe Rogan (Comedian)
Larry David (Writer/Comedian)
Jerry Seinfeld (Writer/Comedian)
Jim Carrey (Actor/Comedian)
Chris Farley (Actor/Comedian)
Roland Jenster (Piano Instructor)
Erin Bro (High School English Teacher)
Mrs. Barker (6th Grade English Teacher)
Coach Hartman (SC Water Polo)
Steven Spielberg (Director)
James Cameron (Director)
Quentin Tarantino (Director)

PREFACE

It was October 21, 2009, when I began my second life on Earth. I was only 20 years old and just two years out of high school when I was "taken by surprise". What happened to me was an extremely rare sequence of events that would ultimately leave me fighting for my life. One moment I was heading to surf the best swell of the year, and the next moment I woke up in a hospital bed as an emaciated patient. What happened to me was so rare that the details of my life-altering situation are still obscure to this day.

When I say I was "taken by surprise", I'm not implying that I was abducted or harmed in a traditional sense but rather my life as I knew it had been abducted. During this period everything went black, what felt like minutes would turn out to have been the better part of a month. I had no idea that loved ones had waited anxiously on pins and needles as I fought for my life. Additionally, I didn't anticipate spending six weeks in an acute rehab facility learning how to walk and talk all over again. Fortunately, I was lucky enough to win the initial battle—and I'm here today to show you how the entire war was won.

My life as I knew it was gone and the likelihood of me ever retrieving anything close to it was a mystery. Before being hospitalized, I was en route for a life that was teeming with possibility. I had dreams that were bigger than myself, and some of them were even coming true. I was on my way to music school, I was in love, I was strong, and I was seemingly unstoppable.

Just when everything seemed so simple and everything was going so well, all hell broke loose. I mean, it's not every day that a young man has a life-threatening stroke before he can legally buy a beer. Furthermore, let's just say that the protocol to save my life nearly took it. The road to recovery and a life of fulfillment has been a windy and arduous process filled with highs and lows, successes and failures.

I have faced countless setbacks and life challenges that broke me in every way imaginable. However, through each of these defeating moments, I have figured out ways to tap into inner strength and fight through the pain, no matter the cost, by declaring to persevere. My "Declaration of Perseverance" is not only my dogfight to survive but my ethos. And it is my gift to you.

This process has never been easy, but I believe choosing the righteous path is the only way. I know that I am extremely fortunate, but it was my mental toughness and unwillingness to plateau that played a major role in combatting my unknown and grim prognosis for recovery. Instead of getting trapped in a mindset of depression, riddled with fear, anxiety, and anger, I figured out how to accept this new challenge and fight to discover new sources of strength and inspiration. I also refused to allow my new heavy reality to define who I am.

In this book, I share my journey of injury, recovery, and reclamation, along with some tips, strategies, and nuggets of wisdom that have helped me throughout this painful and mysterious process. I use the terms "recovery" and "reclamation" interchangeably for specific reasons, which I will explain further throughout this book. I came across most of the lessons I learned throughout the last several years, undoubtedly, the hard way; I want to save as many people as possible from the unnecessary headaches and burdens I endured and show you how to streamline your goals for reclaiming your life post-trauma.

I hope to supply an openhearted account of my experience and a recipe for personal success in your journey. Whether you are a stroke survivor yourself or a loved one of a survivor interested in learning how to cope, this book will help supply the tools to gracefully overcome any trauma that life may throw in your direction.

In the following pages, I will take you on the emotional roller coaster that has been my life over the last 13-plus years and supply you with the tools to powerfully meet any adversity. I hope you find value in my story.

1. MY STORY

The day my life forever changed was known as "Big Wednesday"—at least among the Southern California surf community. It was October 21st, 2009 and Hurricane Rick was headed for the West Coast, pushing 65 mph winds off the tip of Baja, which created ideal conditions for large south swells. The waves had been huge all week and the storm was about to peak on this auspicious "Big Wednesday" morning. To say that excitement was at an all-time high would be an understatement because we had been tracking this swell for days on end.

That morning, while waiting for my good friend Mikey to pick me up, I sat at my piano for a creative writing session. This moment will forever be etched in my mind because although I couldn't have known it at the time, it was the last time I would effortlessly play my piano with both hands. As an aspiring musician, I was on the cusp of taking my music to a more professional level by getting into music school and pursuing my dreams of being a movie score composer. For several weeks, I had been working on a song that I intended to debut at the Musicians Institute in Hollywood, California, and it had a very cinematic vibe.

My brother Bennett was in and out of the family room that morning as I continued to write music on my piano, a vintage baby grand with a wood grain pattern. I vividly remember my brother being very impressed with my song and complimenting me on how "catchy" it sounded. He asked me the name of the song and for whatever reason, I replied, "I call it 'Bad Moon Warrior'." Don't ask me why, it just felt right at the time.

As I transitioned through the chords of my song, my brother made encouraging comments and couldn't seem to get over how "moving" the song was. While it is incredibly difficult to explain the feeling of a song in words, I must say it did have a triumphant and heroic feel. I am not trying to convince anyone that I am some sort of Mozart or Chopin, but I have been told that I have a natural ability to play by ear and write original music. I have always been inspired by how music can influence emotion in the scene of a movie, at a concert, or in the scene of life in general. Looking back at that moment, who would have known that I would be writing the anthem of my life? As inspired as I was to continue playing, it was time to go surf. We couldn't stop talking about how stoked we were to get in the water and how good the surf was going to be, but we had a little time to kill because we were waiting on the tide to rise for ideal conditions.

I vividly remember walking into a juice bar with Mikey as we were eagerly pumping each other up for the surf session soon ahead of us. We walked up to the counter, I backed up just a few steps to look up at the menu, and this is where it all begins. Suddenly, out of nowhere, the menu became distorted and I sort of felt upside down and shook my head. I then turned left to right to scan the room; it too was distorted and warped. Mikey could tell that I was experiencing something strange and quickly asked me if I was OK. I remember I tried to downplay what I was experiencing but still decided to sit down and asked for a glass of water. I remember seeing the glass of water on the table and going to reach for it. The problem was, I was experiencing double vision and was grabbing at an illusion of the glass that was nearly a foot to the right.

Suddenly, my entire left side felt tingly and numb as I slumped deeper into the left side of my chair. Mikey asked me again if I was OK, and I responded, "I'm not sure... I don't know what is happening. I think I'm OK?" At this point, it was obvious that I was far from OK, so Mikey called 911. I remember I still hadn't fully grasped the gravity of the situation, but something was clearly wrong. Within minutes an ambulance arrived, and as it turned out there were some paramedics just one parking lot over. I remember in detail being put through a series of motor skill tests by one of the medics. He said, "Alright, buddy, now push on both of my hands and then squeeze both of my hands, but don't kill me alright... haha!" Well, unfortunately, there was a clear difference in strength levels between my right side and my left side. Though I knew something serious was happening to me, I still had a sense of invincibility. Believe it or not, I was even joking around with the medics as they loaded me onto the gurney.

I distinctly remember the cool morning air on my skin just before they loaded me into the ambulance and shut the doors. The dampening of the sound from the outside world once the doors were tightly shut made me realize how serious this situation was as I suddenly heard the sirens begin to wail on our way to the ER. I'll never forget the abstract thought, "Crap, those sirens are for me." The situation felt surreal more than anything else; I was disoriented but not exactly frightened because I was still thinking and speaking completely coherently.

On the way to the hospital, I continued making light of the situation by saying things like, "This is so lame and the worst timing, I'm supposed to be surfing right now." One of the EMTs chuckled and replied, "I don't know about surfing today, man, but don't worry, it looks like you're going to be fine, you are totally all there and coherent. We just need to get you checked out due to your symptoms." I truly was frustrated and completely bummed out. However, as I'll state again, I clearly did not understand the magnitude of what I was experiencing and, even worse, the direction where everything was headed. What happened next is what truly determined my mortality and it was completely out of my hands.

Little did I know that in contrast to the carefree banter in the ambulance, I would end up spending the better part of a month in a drug-induced coma, unconsciously fighting for my life. I was put under hypothermic treatment, I had tubes coming out of my brain, throat, stomach, and several other parts of my body. Unconsciously, my entire life had been turned inside out.

The Mini Event

Before I dive in any further, I'd like to explain what happened to me roughly three weeks before "Big Wednesday". I had been working two jobs in South Orange County, one as a delivery driver for an Italian restaurant and the other as a barback at a high-end restaurant. I pursued jobs in food and beverage so that my days would be free to attend music school and work on my future. At the time, my 95-year-old grandma lived just a few miles down the road from the music school I would soon be attending. My master plan was to stay in my grandmother's spare room while I went to music school and pursued my dreams. I was fixing up a vintage motorcycle for my journey in LA with the intention of cheating the notorious LA traffic by splitting lanes. In hindsight, this probably wasn't the safest plan in the world, but as an ambitious 20-year-old this was my plan. I had my shortcut to the beach figured out, my side streets to school dialed in, and a fantasy about the life that I intended to live.

My work and social life in Orange County was preparing me for the life I would lead in LA. Getting back to the mini-event, one Friday night I had a particularly late evening with friends that left me feeling more tired than usual in the morning. After a few cups of coffee, I walked into the backyard and experienced the strangest sensation - my vision was distorted and I felt disoriented. My girlfriend at the time asked me if I was OK, to which I replied, "I'm not exactly sure... " I did not realize it at the time, but what I was experiencing was a TIA (transient ischemic attack). This is the body's way of sending a warning signal indicating that there is something neurologically off. Unfortunately, having no idea what was going on, I just figured it was possibly a hangover and maybe a little too much caffeine. My reaction was to drink a bunch of water to try and rehydrate, take an aspirin, and take a nap to help calm my nerves. Once I woke up, I felt 100% myself again and went about my life as if nothing ever happened, which obviously was not the right call. I will never forget waking up from that nap feeling so relieved this weird sensation had worn off and walking straight over to my piano to work on a couple of songs I was writing. I had a particularly powerful piano session that day, as my transition to music school was growing ever closer.

To this day, I wish I had been aware of how serious that warning signal of the visual abnormalities was because I might have gone to the hospital for a CAT scan to see if there was some sort of "ticking time bomb" hanging out in my brain. Unfortunately, that's not what happened. This so-called "mini event" was my brain's way of telling me to seek medical attention ASAP because of a dissection blocking blood flow to the right occipital lobe of my brain. Being a young and healthy 20-year-old, neither my family nor myself assumed I was on the brink of experiencing a stroke. Put simply, this was a massive lesson learned and I am all too aware that my entire life could be entirely different today had I known what to do. There is an old saying, "If you listen to your body when it whispers, you won't have to hear it scream." In this case, I was too naïve to understand the whisper.

The Event

I would like to circle back to October 21, 2009, which was approximately two weeks after the "mini event". While in the ambulance, I was in absolute denial and awe that I was having a dire situation; it simply didn't feel real. It was an out-of-body experience that felt like I was examining my own existence through a microscope. Everything around me felt dampened, non-existent, and gone. Suddenly, we reached the hospital doors.

Still feeling these strange side effects, the medics rushed me out of the ambulance and into the cool morning air. Within seconds, I was rushed to the ER. Being admitted into the hospital is a bizarre and surreal experience no matter what, but I still had an overwhelming sense of, "I know I'm going to be OK, I just need this to be over now." I still cannot pinpoint why I had this overwhelming sense of confidence, but I can only assume it was denial, naïveté, or possibly my subconscious giving me a clue that, no matter how devastating the outcome, I will figure out a way to work through everything. I would like to believe it was the latter of those intuitions.

Upon entry to the ER, I had zero wait time, probably because of the seemingly crucial nature of my situation; therefore, I bypassed the always eerie group of sick or injured people waiting their turn for medical attention in the ER waiting room. I was then wheeled into a side room where I was put through further motor skill and vision testing to try and determine what was going on with me. By this time my parents, brothers, and our long-time family doctor were there with me as I was being put through a series of further testing. I was also put through a CAT scan, which is essentially an X-ray of your brain. At first, it showed nothing alarming.

I continued working with a neurologist, who determined after several tests (lasting roughly an hour) that my symptoms appeared to be improving. Put simply, he said that he believed I was going to be fine and I would probably be discharged later that day, or worst case scenario I would be kept for one night and continue to be monitored. This was great news obviously for a multitude of reasons but especially because we were gearing up to go on our annual surf trip for my dad's birthday in Santa Barbara the following weekend. It may sound insane given the nature of everything that followed, but I specifically remember asking the neurologist if I would be able to surf the following weekend because at that moment we were getting reassurances that my symptoms were seemingly temporary.

All of a sudden, a swarm of doctors and nurses flooded my room, creating a sense of panic and emergency. "We found a blood clot in his brain and it needs to be removed immediately!" My family, the neurologist, and myself were all confused by the panic because out of nowhere surgery had become a topic of discussion. Shortly thereafter, the situation was escalated by surgeons saying, "We need to rush him into the OR now!" and "Time is brain! Time is brain!" The next moments of my life become a bit of a blur, but I remember being rushed through hallways and watching the lights above flying by at an urgent speed. Bennett walked alongside the gurney and ran his hand through my hair, telling me, "Everything is going to be OK." just moments before they shaved my head for surgery.

The foot of the gurney blasted through the OR doors. Suddenly, I felt panic and chaos oddly intermixed with calmness. Beams of blue light and unexplainable sensations of every thought and emotion I have ever known all swirled together into one unit of confusion, mixed with a dreamlike tranquility.

Now everything is calm and quiet as I snap into a ridged reality in a sterile environment, a very different reality from what I had been experiencing previously. I can hear family members asking me to count to five with my right hand. "Count to five using your right hand, Kevin. One, two, three, four, five." Then a voice asks me to throw a peace sign, then a hang loose sign, which was followed by an eruption of cheering, laughter, and tears. I had no clue at the time, but nearly a month had passed and these were little tests given by loved ones and nurses to figure out how much of me was still intact. Mind you, I had no ability to speak and I couldn't tell you if my eyes were open or closed.

Whenever brain surgery is performed, the patient is awake on the operating table. While I don't remember every nuance of what I'm about to tell you, I do have some strong recollections of moments during the surgery. Essentially, one doctor made a risky decision to rush me into surgery to remove what they believed was a clot in an artery of my brain, located in the right occipital lobe. What they did not take into account was that the blockage was not a blood clot but rather a dissection of the interior wall of the artery. What the procedure called for was the insertion of a catheter into my groin, which led a pathway into my femoral vein, bypassed my lungs and the heart, and eventually made its way into the carotid artery, which finally allowed access to the affected area of my brain.

Once they located the correct area of my brain, a device called the "mercy tool" was fed through the catheter, and efforts were made to remove the alleged clot. The tool looks a lot like a thin metal wire, and it is the job of the neurosurgeon to "pierce" the clot with the wire and make a corkscrew knot on the other side of the clot to try and pull it into the catheter, thus removing it from the artery entirely.

However, upon entry, the artery in my brain ruptured, causing an intracranial bleed that nearly cost me my life right then and there. While on the operating table, as soon as the bleed was created, I lurched up and vomited everywhere. I tried to jump off the table but was restrained as they tried to fix the damage and stop the bleeding. Any blockage to an artery in the brain is a very serious matter, but the rupturing of an artery causing a brain bleed is far worse and often fatal. I was just millimeters away from being a roast duck, which is precisely why this procedure was a very risky one. Let's just say, I am very lucky to be alive.

I will never know for sure, but I believe my heart stopped that day and I was revived via paddle shock to my heart through electrical cardioversion. There are two reasons I hold this belief. Firstly, I experienced a series of events that I can only explain as giving me a feeling of "crossing over". Beams of blue light, the feeling of being sucked through a wormhole, and even rapid hallucinations of being an infant. Maybe this was my life flashing before my eyes, as they say? It was like a tug-of-war between the world as I knew it and this vast pasture of the uncharted universe. This was a life experience that is difficult to translate into words, but that is about as well as I can briefly describe the experience on paper.

The other reason is that my dad noticed two rectangle-shaped bruises on my chest while I lay unconscious in a coma, and they were never explained. I had not experienced any trauma to my chest or ribs, so there was simply no reason for the odd bruising. To this day, the only thing that makes sense is that I had a near-death experience.

I wouldn't be telling the truth if I said I didn't wish things happened differently that day and that the procedure was a success, but I have no bad blood or ill will toward anyone regarding what happened to me. I'm just grateful I survived at all and that I'm alive today. Hospitals, surgeons, and the entire medical industry are put in place to help us when we are sick and injured. I truly believe the majority of medical professionals do everything in their power for their patient's best interests. However, we are all human and we are all flawed. Even the smartest and most talented medical professionals are capable of making mistakes.

The worst part about this whole experience is the guilt I felt for putting my family, friends, and loved ones through such a terrifyingly chaotic and unknown experience. Now I know that may sound insane given what I was going through at the time, but you have to understand, there was an entire month where I was completely out of commission and no one knew what the outcome of this whole thing would look like.

No one—neither doctors nor ICU nurses nor neuro experts —could predict what was going to happen to me. The area of my brain that was affected indicated a vast array of potential complications and cognitive damage; however, nobody knew exactly to what extent. The only thing that they really could see was that there was still brain activity. But it was unknown what exactly that activity would look like once I woke up. Putting my parents and all my loved ones through all that still irritates me. I wish I could have traveled through time, at least to the moment I was awake, to put everyone at ease. To let everyone know that I was not going to die and that I would ultimately pull through and make an unexpected recovery. But, unfortunately, that was not my reality, and everyone had to sit on the edge of their seats in emotional agony, awaiting the unknown results of my brain trauma. That is a level of angst I do not wish upon my worst enemy.

The Coma

I have received countless questions about what it was like to be in a coma for nearly a month. All I can do is try my best to explain what my personal experience was like.

I should probably first note that I was in a combination of a drug-induced coma along with hypothermic treatment. The high volume of medication I was administered was to keep me in a comatose state, and the hypothermic treatment was administered to lower my core body temperature to reduce brain swelling and prevent further damage. I was placed on a ventilator, with several tubes draining fluid from my skull. Several other tubes, wires, and medical devices were connected to the rest of my body to keep me alive. IVs, PICC lines, a catheter, and a G.I. tube, which went directly through the abdomen, through the abdominal muscles and stomach lining, and into the stomach.

I would later learn that there were several moments where it was thought that I was not going to make it. These life-threatening moments occurred mainly when my brain swelling would get to a dangerous level, and many times doctors were preparing to perform a craniectomy, which is where surgeons remove part of the skull when brain swelling becomes dangerous and poses a threat to survival. Usually, the swelling would occur when I was agitated and my brain/cranial pressure would increase to a near-fatal level or at the very least dangerously close to further brain damage. Luckily, some of the more skilled ICU nurses would come to my rescue and make sure my cranial pressure levels came down by rotating certain dials on the machine I was hooked up to, releasing medication, and reducing swelling. It is no exaggeration when I say that some of those angels in the ICU saved my life on multiple occasions. Being kept alive by the hands of another person is an indescribable feeling. The level of gratitude I have for those nurses is infinite. Without them, I would surely be a goner.

One of the questions I get asked the most is whether I could hear my family members and friends speaking to me while I was under. The answer is yes; however, my experience was different from other stories I have heard about people being in a coma. For me, I could hear people speaking to me, but it would essentially create a surreal reality in my mind, where I was fully engaging in conversation or whatever activity my imagination created. I could hear the voices, but it wasn't like I was aware that I was in a hospital bed, in a coma, and couldn't respond. I have heard other stories of people who are in a coma and can hear people talking to them. They want to respond, but they can't because they are trapped in a coma. My experience was much different, for instance: In one of the scenarios I could hear my dad speaking to me and I thought we were full-on having a conversation upstairs in my parent's master bedroom while he was getting ready for work. I remember specifically that he was wearing his typical business attire, a white button-down dress shirt, with some tie, and slacks, and he was shaving while we were casually chatting. That is how vivid some of my coma dreams were when I could hear someone's voice. Our conversation wasn't particularly deep, just our typical father–son small talk about our day, such as my preparation for music school and the new deals he was working on. It was so realistic that to this day it almost feels like it took place. I could even smell the scent of my parent's master bedroom and the Old Spice cologne my dad would wear. Even the time of day seemed precise—the morning sun peeking through a small window above the master bathroom—just to give you a little perspective on how realistic this all seemed to me.

Another bizarre coma dream occurred when I could hear my friend Shane in the hospital room. I had the most vivid dream where I was racing my vintage motorcycle down the freeway in order to get to his front door in time to save a kitten in a box from the summer heat. I know this sounds bizarre, but the association with my friend's voice triggered a fictitious narrative in the subconscious mind.

I also had many dreams of trying to save certain friends from getting into fights and getting hurt. In most of these dreams, I was going out of my way and often putting myself at risk to help others, which is subconsciously true but was certainly expressed in a surreal state. I'm not going to go into detail about every little nuance of every dream because that would be like trying to explain a Quentin Tarantino movie from start to finish. All I can say is that everything was very bizarre but also very realistic, and it felt like I went through a time warp. The coma lasted for a month but felt like a few minutes, at the same time it seemed to last an eternity.

When it comes to those dreams of me going out of my way to be the hero, I can only assume that my mind and spirit were subconsciously aware of my actual reality. Because, at that moment, I was the one who really needed saving. I honestly feel like I created these scenarios in my subconscious because deep down I knew that I was in dire straits. I understand that very little of this may make any sense, but I'm only painting a small picture of how bizarre it was to be in a coma for that long.

When they finally brought me out of the coma, I had extremely intense hallucinations. In the first one I can remember, I had green hair and I was in the hospital because I hit my head skateboarding with professional skateboarder Danny Way. I have never even met the man, but for some reason, that's what I thought. I also thought that I was on the Spice Girls' tour plane for lord knows what reason. From what I understand, these hallucinations were largely the result of me coming off the extraordinary amount of medication that I was given over the previous few weeks.

In order to keep me sedated for the duration of the induced coma, I was given just below the lethal dosage of fentanyl, morphine, and a litany of other medications. When the brain has sustained the level of trauma and swelling that mine had, it is crucial to keep the patient and their brain activity as relaxed as possible in order for the swelling to subside, allowing the brain to begin healing. Apparently, in my case, my metabolism was processing the meds so rapidly that I had enough in me to put down a horse. I'm not sure how accurate that is, but that's what one doctor jokingly told me. Nonetheless, I'm fortunate enough to have survived—and survive the heavy doses of medication needed to keep me asleep. I'm highlighting this because it took several weeks for me to detox off all the heavy sedatives and I had to receive shots of methadone in my abdomen multiple times a day. The feeling of detoxing from heavy opioids is not something I would wish upon my worst enemy. Especially when you are bound to a hospital bed. It felt like my skin was crawling and I wanted to throw my bed out the window, yet I was a prisoner to the bed.

With my right hand, I tried yanking out all of the tubes I was connected to, including my tracheotomy tube, which obviously would not have been good. The tracheotomy tube was no longer hooked up to the ventilator, but because I contracted pneumonia, they left a small tube inserted into my neck with a cap. I was too weak in the initial phases to cough out the fluid in my lungs from pneumonia, so they would slide a little catheter tube down the tracheotomy site to vacuum out the fluid buildup residing in my lungs. Having your lungs vacuumed out feels about how you would imagine: absolutely horrifying. The worst part of it all is that along with the fluid being vacuumed out, it also sucks out any oxygen in your lungs. So it felt like I was being buried alive for several moments at a time. Anyway, there were clearly several reasons behind my agitation and discomfort, hence my multiple attempts to pull out all my IVs and other medical devices. It was for this behavior that they had to tie my right wrist to the bed. They only needed to tie my right wrist, as my entire left side was completely paralyzed; therefore, my left arm and hand were not a threat. In my mind, I felt completely restrained, helpless, and tied to a hospital bed, which created a level of anger and anxiety you can only imagine.

I would like to take a moment and add all this up because I actually haven't thought deeply about any of this for a long time and have probably blocked it out for a good reason. So I'm coming off the heaviest drugs available on earth, getting methadone shots in my abdomen to try and keep me at ease,

I'm paralyzed on the entire left side of my body, 50% blind, soiling myself in a diaper, having my lungs vacuumed out and feeling suffocated, and I'm physically tied down on only my functioning limbs. This is a psychological nightmare and an absolute mental war zone. This entire experience was pure torture and there was absolutely nothing I could do about it. I should also note that because of my tracheotomy tube, I was not allowed any water, not even ice chips. So I had already spent a month having not one sip of water, then spent the following two weeks being refused even a drop of water to quench my thirst.

I remember vividly when they finally gave me what is called a "swab". Basically, it's a damp sponge on a lollipop stick that they give you so that your tongue doesn't stick to the roof of your mouth like Velcro. I must have gone through 30 of those swabs a day during those two weeks of water deprivation. I also was not allowed any food as they were not sure how my swallowing mechanism was going to react.

For the prevention of choking, they kept me hydrated through IV and fed me through my G.I. stomach tube. Even when my body was being hydrated through IV, my thirst was never quenched, and being fed through a G.I. tube did not satisfy my hunger. It basically just feels like you're being starved to death and dying of thirst simultaneously. Finally, after two weeks, I was finally allowed to drink water again. The nurses tried to ration it, but I chugged as much as my stomach could handle. I'll never forget the feeling of gulping cold water - it was the most thirst-quenching satisfaction I have ever experienced. However, I was also irritated because I knew I could swallow water the entire time, but the hospital wouldn't allow it. I understand hospital protocol and liability, but I just wish there were some exceptions, such as trying to see if I could swallow so that I wasn't deprived of water and food for so long.

Initial Recovery

I suppose everything leading up to this point was part of the initial recovery, but eventually, they began putting me through the initial phases of actual physical therapy. Step one was to simply get me to sit up in bed for 10 seconds. At this point, I had lost nearly 60 pounds and I was a skeletal shell of my former self. I had lost all my abdominal muscles and core strength, so it felt like an infant trying to establish their posture for the first time. The frustration of this weak feeling inspired me to achieve the 10-second goal. Shortly thereafter we toyed with a 20-second goal, then a 30-second goal, until I was able to successfully sit upright on my own without any assistance. If I recall correctly, this took roughly a week of what felt like running a daily marathon, but it was just sitting in an upright position for a few moments at a time to strengthen my core. I always find it interesting when I see a show on TV where someone wakes up from being in a coma and they just pop up as if there hasn't been a significant level of muscle atrophy.

Once I was able to sit up on my own after about a week, they eventually prepared me for the next phase of therapy, which was learning how to swallow and use my vocal cords since my esophagus was inactive for nearly a month. To put this into perspective, I was awake for nearly a week and I was only communicating through eye contact and primitive sign language with my unafflicted right hand. The sensation of swallowing for the first time was odd, to say the least, but as I said earlier, my first sip of water gave me a feeling of absolute euphoria and bliss. You never realize that some of the most basic human functions can be taken for granted, and I will never forget the satisfaction of simply quenching my thirst for the first time in what felt like an eternity.

The next task was to get me to speak. I worked with a speech therapist, who would come by every day and train me to use my vocal cords again. It sounds elementary, but we went over simple exercises like training with vowels and simply relearning the basics of how words are phrased and how they sound. I will never forget hearing the initial sound of my voice. It was unrecognizable to me, in fact, it sounded like I had inhaled helium from a balloon. It was a humorous situation but also a sobering reality check. Speaking became as easy as chewing gum, and in a short period of time, I developed my voice and could communicate clearly. It was at this point that I was able to prove that I had not sustained any cognitive deficit because I could communicate as well as I did before. I was also able to get more verbally involved with the next phases of my recovery because I was no longer mute.

Attempting to stand up was the next big challenge. I am not exaggerating in the slightest when I say this was the most difficult thing I have ever experienced, both physically and mentally. It felt like I was trying to lift a thousand pounds sitting on my shoulders, and it took every bit of my might just to fully stand for five seconds. I looked and felt exactly like Bambi when he is learning to stand and walk for the first time. My mind was under the impression that I could just stand up with no problem. However, the week prior I could barely sit up on my own, so I should have known better. I was using a device that looks like an extended walker to hold onto and pull myself up onto my feet, of course being spotted by several physical therapists. Beads of sweat combined with tears ran down my face, followed by shock and even a little laughter as I was finally able to stand on my feet. It took two weeks just to stand, so I couldn't even imagine the thought of walking which was destined for my near future.

Once I reached this level of recovery, I was transferred to another hospital for acute rehab. This is where they put me through a more vigorous routine to prepare me for discharge from the hospital. I was still so weak at this point that I was still reliant on a diaper and a bedpan to go to the bathroom. Phase one of my rehabilitation routine at this acute rehab was the most difficult and humiliating phase, and it involved getting rid of the bedpan, urinal, and diaper, all while learning how to use the bathroom again. It's basically like being potty trained, but I was weaker and even less coordinated than a toddler. This was a major adjustment and an extremely humbling life experience. Several nights of wetting the bed, hitting the nurse's button for assistance to use the restroom, and needing help became my reality.

One of the most terrifying reality checks I had through this entire experience was seeing myself in the mirror for the first time. I'll never forget it. It was after being helped to use the restroom, and I was wheeled over to the sink to wash my hands. Bennett was with me and I could tell he didn't want me to see my reflection in the mirror. But I reluctantly looked up and saw myself. I didn't even recognize the person in the mirror. I looked like a skeleton and had a massive hole in the front of my throat, with a tube sticking out. My jaw dropped, a flood of every emotion imaginable overwhelmed me, and it was absolutely a devastating blow to my spirit. It all became so real and I was completely speechless. I felt violated, frustrated, sad, angry, and broken.

I simply wanted it all to just go away, but this was my life and I had to face it. I had plenty of positive guidance, love, and support from my family, but I'd be fibbing if I didn't find it initially difficult to look on the bright side. Of course, my rehab doctor and nurses tried to reassure me that things would get better, but sometimes it's hard to see the forest beyond the trees. Shout out to Dr. Lynn, who was my head rehab doctor at the acute rehabilitation center. He along with the medical team assured me that in time I would gain my muscle back and get to a healthy weight. I was told that, eventually, the tracheotomy hole would close on its own and the holes in my head from where the tubes to relieve cranial pressure were would heal. I just had no clue about the level of discipline and work I had ahead of me. Seeing my reflection in the mirror was just the tip of the iceberg. There were several more icebergs soon to follow. My reality at this point was that I had very little control. There were a few things I could control, such as narrowing down my medication and controlling my nutrition, which felt like minor victories.

After about the third or fourth time waking up in the middle of the night from wetting the bed, I started to become extremely concerned that this was some sort of additional side effect from my brain injury. I specifically remember talking to my doctor about it, and he explained to me that sometimes when a patient is reliant on a catheter, a diaper, or both, it can take some time for your body to adjust, therefore bedwetting is considered normal. But something still did not seem right and I did not feel like myself. I was irritable, anxious, and depressed, and while this all may seem justifiable given what I had just gone through, I could still tell something was off, even outside of the obvious. I was being given a small cup full of pills several times a day and I wasn't even sure what I was taking, what it was for, or what the effects of these medications were. I had this sneaking suspicion that something I was taking was causing me to sleep, even though I was pissing the bed, and it was making me feel suicidal, so I asked my doctor specifically what pharmaceuticals I was taking multiple times a day.

Here is the list, just to name a few:

- Keppra (focal seizure medication)
- Seroquel (antipsychotic medication)
- Baclofen (muscle relaxant)

- Methadone (shot in the abdomen twice a day. This was used to taper me off fentanyl)
- Sleeping medication
- Statins (blood pressure medication)

Just in case you are unaware of what all of these medications are, these are all pharmaceutical-grade sedatives (except for the blood pressure meds, but those can still make you drowsy), so no wonder I wasn't waking up to use the restroom! I refused all the medications that were not necessary as soon as I got the list, and when they tried to talk me into taking those meds, I politely told them to kick rocks. They even sent in a psychologist to evaluate me for several weeks to see if I was doing OK or if I felt like I was "crawling out of my skin". It was actually quite the opposite, as soon as I got off all those meds I felt completely liberated and actually started to feel like myself again. Before this moment, I had a very hard time laughing or even cracking a smile, and those who know me know I love to laugh and have a light-hearted sense of humor. I felt like the unnecessary meds were causing a major piece of me to feel missing and I was right. Before I refused those medications, there were several moments where I made suicidal comments and actually meant them. Before the stroke happened, I was full of life, ambition, motivation, athletic, and an aspiring musician. So, to be in this downer state of mind was extremely foreign to me.

Although I had obviously been put through the wringer up until this point, I could still feel that these dark thoughts of not wanting to exist and this deep depression were coming from another source outside of my reality. The good news is, I finally narrowed it down to the mixture of medication I was being given, and as soon as I eradicated it from my daily protocol, l was actually able to laugh again and feel motivated to get to work on my new voyage ahead. Oh, and—big surprise—the bedwetting stopped immediately and never happened again.

I want to clarify that I am not a physician, nor am I giving medical advice. There are times when the aforementioned medications are absolutely necessary for certain individuals, but in my unique case, the cocktail had become detrimental to my psyche and was no longer serving me. I was already devastated that this situation had happened to me, and to put it succinctly, the procedure to save my life ironically almost took my life. So, in putting the pieces back together they prescribed me antipsychotics and "don't kill yourself pills". I was also on sedatives, which just made me feel tired, lame, and stupid. Not ideal for trying to rehabilitate me mentally and physically.

Having this new revived sense of myself again, I was finally able to get a better grasp on what I was experiencing, for better and for worse. The drugs I had just pulled off of, although a crucial step to snapping back into myself again, did suppress some degree of fear which was now present. I would often wake up in the middle of the night in a panic, fearful of the unknown future for me, Sweating and scared, sometimes I was up for a couple hours trying to make sense of everything. That is, until I had possibly the most profound spiritual experience of my life. I remember it like it happened last night. I was sound asleep in my hospital bed, when I was awakened by the most warm and comforting feeling. At first, I thought it was part of a bizarre dream, but I lifted my head up and scanned the room to realize that I was very much awake and alert. The best way I can describe this feeling is like when you enter a perfectly heated jacuzzi on a cool night. As you slowly enter the warm water, your body and mind is flooded with incredible comfort that gives you goosebumps from head to toe. However, I was in a hospital bed and there certainly was no jacuzzi in sight. So why was I experiencing this amazing sensation out of thin air? I continued to look around the room and at this point I was almost slightly on edge because I could not figure out why I was feeling this way. That is until it all became abundantly clear. I will never forget, I looked up at the clock on the wall at the foot of my bed which indicated it was 3:33am, and when I looked back down at the foot of my bed, there stood a figure. It was sort of unclear at first but then cleared up in my minds eye. As this presence became clearer and clearer, I could make out who this visitor was. A pretty brunette woman wearing a light yellow sundress with bright white teeth and a comforting smile. It was my Aunt Charlene, who I've never met because she had unfortunately passed away not too long before I was born. Still in shock but not scared, I was just frozen wondering what on earth was happening. It was at that moment she slightly tilted her head, and gave me this look of, what I can only describe as absolute reassurance, that everything was going to be okay and I was going to make it through this challenge and have a life well lived. There were no actual words spoken between us, yet more of a telepathic exchange. This whole experience was so remarkable and is not something that I really talk about. In fact, I originally wasn't going to write about it at all. However, as I have relived my whole experience through the writing process, I felt it would be remiss to leave such an extremely profound piece of the story out. It was truly life changing and completely shifted my perception and my course of action for the better. I understand this can be a touchy subject for some, but the truth is that I feel like Aunt Charlene came through that early morning to give me strength and reassurance the everything was going to work out. Call it what you want, she was there for me as a guardian angel, a spirit guide, or whatever phrasing best explains this phenomenon. Until we meet again Aunt Charlene...

Coming back around to the physical therapy aspect, I had been on all those medications from the very start. So learning how to walk again and use my left side felt almost impossible because I could barely wake up in the morning and I felt extremely sluggish. Once I had finally been pulled off all those sedatives, my daily energy levels were significantly higher and therefore gave me hope and inspiration to keep pushing forward. I was determined to walk, and I remember that I had my brother bring me a pair of my favorite Vans skate shoes, which were the first shoes that I put on my feet since the accident. I remember that these particular shoes were forest green and a little beat up from a lot of skateboarding, but sliding them on was like a reminder of who I was. Almost like the satisfaction of seeing an old friend or visiting your home town. I hate to keep referring to certain experiences as "hard to put into words", but this was a big one. The feeling of taking my first step nearly 6-weeks post waking up from a coma was truly indescribable. It was like a weird mixture of fear and embarrassment, mixed with a massive amount of eagerness and hope. When it came to relearning how to walk, they put a gait belt around my torso so they could spot me as I attempted to walk with a walking device. Normally they give you a typical walker that you might see some elderly folks using, but because I had zero function in my left arm and hand, I had only my right hand to rely on for support. The crutch looked a lot like a saw horse made out of aluminum, with lightweight rods and rubber caps so it would not slide on the ground. I had foot drop, which means I could not lift the front part of my foot up (zero dorsiflexion), nor did I have any plantar flexion, so I could not push off of my left foot at all. My ankle had zero function, so it felt like a dead fish attached to my leg flopping around. Essentially, they trained my left knee to remain locked so I could swing it around in front of me and then use my right leg to step forward. They would have me walk slowly up and down the hallways of the hospital until I became too fatigued, which could become dangerous and lead to a fall. The last thing I needed was an additional injury. I remember being in the physical therapy room doing several exercises with resistance bands, light weights, and other acute rehabilitation equipment. For example, things you might witness in a preschool classroom, like brightly colored blocks and tic-tac-toe board games test fine motor and basic mental abilities. For the record, this was one of the more humbling aspects of the severity of my brain trauma. They also worked with the paralysis of my left arm and hand, but my side effects in that department were so severe there was only so much they could do. This was also back in 2009, so stroke rehabilitation has come a long way since then. Rehab protocol has had some much-needed improvement and it is still in ongoing phases of improvement.

All of this physical therapy was outrageously exhausting and, at many times, discouraging and depressing, but no form of rehab was more taxing on my psyche than occupational/visual rehabilitation. This is the area of brain damage that is least predictable when it comes to restoration. For certain stroke survivors like myself, the area of the brain responsible for vision is compromised. In my case, the right occipital lobe was affected, which in turn led to partial left-side blindness. I have a 50% left-side visual field cut, which means the damage sustained to that area of my brain resulted in a 90-degree range of vision, whereas before I had the full 180-degree range as most people do. For those who do experience vision loss as a side effect, the potential return of vision can be a tricky one. Some may have their vision return to normal soon after the incident, some have visual improvements months or even years down the line, and for some, their vision is never "fully" restored.

Even from the very beginning, I've had a "never quit" mentality and I have had faith in my ability to physically recover. If there's one thing I can say, I truly believed that I would get everything back and nothing could stop me. However, losing 50% of my left visual field has always deeply bothered me. Beyond the weird limp, beyond my arm and hand dancing around with minds of their own, and seeing people notice my side effects, the vision loss was always the worst part for me. I've always had the mentality of kicking ass all the way to full functionality, but I could not will my vision to return 100%. I prayed for it, meditated deeply on it, and wished for it with every form of hope in between. It took a lot of time and it took a lot of patience, but throughout this whole process, I have without a doubt made major visual improvements. I spent countless hours trying to develop new and innovative exercises to restore my vision and discovered new ways of exercising that area of my brain in an attempt to wake up new neural pathways to restore my visual field.

At this point in time I have been going through rigorous physical and mental therapy and slowly inching toward my discharge date from the hospital. I'm now at nearly two months of hospitalization and extremely eager to leave this place and never look back. It is now mid-December and I am finally "recovered" to a point where the hospital will discharge me and let me go home. A quick side note: As I mentioned earlier, I spent my 21st birthday in a coma. My birthday is November 8th, and I was sure I'd be home at least in time for Thanksgiving, which my family hosts every year, so it is something we all really look forward to. Unfortunately, that was wishful thinking and I spent Thanksgiving in the hospital that year, while everybody celebrated at my parents' house. I missed out on one of the greatest celebrations of Thanksgiving yet, mainly because everyone was celebrating their thanks for not only my survival but for the fact that, even though my road to recovery was sure to be very long and rocky, it appeared that I was going to be OK. I too was thankful. I remember calling my parents' house while alone in my wheelchair at the hospital, and I was put on the speaker to hear everyone cheering and congratulating me on my survival. My little cousin, Ella, who was only 5 or 6 at the time grabbed the phone and told me she loved me, and I'll never forget that emotional rush. It all became so clear, what I had just gone through and what I was currently experiencing. It was the most present I had ever felt, and for the first time in a very long time, tears flooded uncontrollably down my face while I sat silently in my wheelchair. They were happy tears but also tears of acknowledgment for my new unknown. Doing everything in my power to choke back more tears, I was barely able to respond with, "I love you too." I'm typically not that emotional of a person, but that one really got me. The sound of her sweet little voice innocently expressing her love for me in the purest and most authentic way. Although little ones are unaware of this gift, it's almost a superpower kids can have. This became another compounding moment where I began to pick up more strength.

I also had some visitors that day; small groups of my family would come by the hospital and visit with some of my favorite dishes, which was nice. I hadn't had chewable food in what felt like forever, so to say this was enjoyable is an understatement.

After Thanksgiving had passed, we were now rapidly approaching Christmas, and I said to my doctor, "There is no way in hell I'm staying in here through the entire holiday season and missing Christmas." He chuckled and said if I did everything I was supposed to do in my acute rehab, the hospital should be able to get me out of there before Christmas. Luckily, I did my part and was discharged just before Christmas and got to spend Christmas at home.

Recovery At Home

While being released from the hospital and finally getting home put me in a state of euphoria you can't imagine, however, my battle was far from over.

Call it wishful thinking, but nobody, let alone myself, could have predicted the long journey ahead I was about to embark on. Now, I've had some incredible doctors and therapists who had given me hope, strength, and light at the end of the tunnel as far as how my recovery would potentially turn out, but I had an equal amount of naysayers and negative feedback. Many medical professionals would ultimately give me a grim and overly harsh prognosis for recovery. I'm not exactly sure what the purpose of scaring the crap out of the patient would be, but if medical professionals or a fellow patient attempted to tell me what I was incapable of, I would simply disregard that person. I found out pretty early on that these people can only cause harm in my recovery, so I removed them from my life. I suppose it is possible that the negative feedback gave me some level of strength, almost like a "watch me prove you wrong" (and I have), but I do not think any of these folks deserve that level of credit. I'm just fortunate enough to have thick skin and mental toughness that allowed me to break through the negativity and not allow these words of discouragement to negatively impact my path of reclamation.

I don't want to make this depressing or angering, but one of the first things I was told by a neurologist (and I won't mention any names) was that I would never be able to play music again. Hearing this for the first time absolutely shattered my world and ruined any bit of hope I was holding onto for a future in music. This same character told me that I would most likely never surf again or have the ability to walk on my own without some sort of crutch, like a walker or a cane. Again, I'm not exactly sure why any doctor would throw such a horrifying and just depressing prognosis for recovery at their patient, but I had already suffered enough. I narrowly escaped the clutches of death and all I had left was my hope and faith in my abilities. In your darkest hour, when you absolutely hit rock bottom and you feel depressed beyond comprehension, I don't find it constructive to strip a person of the only thing they have left: faith in themselves.

Now, hitting rock bottom is typically pretty scary and most certainly very uncomfortable. However, I have come to the conclusion that as important as it is to find solutions and push off the rocky bottom toward the surface, it is equally important to analyze the darkness and look around for a moment. Don't be so quick to come up for air, because the most powerful forms of strength and value are found in these undesired circumstances. Much like the most highly sought-after resources of our time. Things like diamonds and precious metals are created and formed under the harshest conditions and the most intense pressure that Earth has to offer. I eventually found the light within the depths of this nightmare and capitalized on those harsh lessons learned. It took time, but eventually, with the help of another fantastic neurologist, I began to realize that I had a bit more control over the outcome of my trauma than others had previously stated.

As far as at-home physical therapy goes, this was your basic, run-of-the-mill, insurance-covered physical therapy, where they offer you 12 in-home sessions and then you are completely on your own. Due to the difficulty of transferring patients from car to facility, they make this effort somewhat convenient, but I knew it was swiftly going to come to an end and I would eventually have to take my recovery into my own hands. So they brought the equipment to my home and put me through exercises where I really began to improve. It was so slow and so frustrating, but I knew I had to do it in order to progress. I believe the at-home therapy went on for about three weeks until I was transferred to outpatient rehab, where a family member would drive me to physical therapy and I would continue with their protocol for physical therapy. I absolutely hated it, as much as I looked forward to it because it got me out of the house and gave me something to do. I got myself in trouble multiple times for pushing myself "too far". I would do everything in my power to assure them I was capable of taking these exercises a few steps further, but they explained that because of liability they could not allow it. I began to realize that I was pushing my progress because at times I felt like they were unintentionally holding me back. I have never blamed anyone for this as it is simply professionals sticking to their education and training. These are extremely valuable players in the process of recovery, but never forget that the deepest level of understanding and knowledge comes from the individual patient living the experience.

This next part is bittersweet, mainly because my insurance eventually ran out and they stopped covering my physical therapy. I think it is safe to say that everyone would agree it takes a lot longer than four weeks to recover from a stroke or traumatic brain injury. They do everything in their power in physical therapy to "prepare you for life" post-trauma; however, their window for preparing patients is entirely too small. So I refer to this as bittersweet because, while my coverage reaching its limits was bitter, sweetness came from the magic of at-home physical therapy being taken into my own hands.

First of all, I cannot thank my family and friends enough for the incredible support they provided me. Even after outpatient rehab and multiple sessions of physical therapy, I still could not do most of the things we all take for granted on a daily basis. Things like tying my shoes, going to the bathroom by myself, showering by myself, shaving, and grooming myself, just to name a few. For example, I find long nails to be disgusting, and clipping them on my own was seemingly impossible, so I needed help with literally everything, right down to nail trimming. Going to the restroom was yet another embarrassing thing I needed daily help with as my body's core strength was still not fully recovered and my balance was still way off, so you can use your imagination for how difficult that might be.

Anyway, I'd like to get into the topic of therapy at home and how I started stumbling across new and innovative tactics for improving not only my physical well-being but my state of mind as well. I began to realize early on the importance of having the proper mindset and attitude going into my physical therapy. I cannot stress enough how crucial this part of the equation is if you're looking to get the best possible results out of your recovery. It takes a certain level of thinking in order to attack your physical training with the utmost strength and intent. Without this mental preparation and psychological strengthening, you will never get the most out of your training and most likely dread training altogether. Dreading physical therapy and training is a dangerous path and will only lead to plateaus that ultimately hold us back.

Something that really stood out to me when I began going to the public gym again and started to approach training there is that a lot of people speak about going to the gym as if it is a burden or some sort of taxing chore. We often hear, "Oh, I have to get the gym out of the way," or, "I can't wait to just be done with my workout so I can just chill." This is also a terrible way to approach physical fitness for anyone, especially someone who is in a state of physical and mental recovery.

Instead of viewing my training as some sort of annoying task that gets in the way of my leisure activities, I chose to view my physical therapy as a celebration of my capabilities. It is without a doubt a celebration of life to be able to move our bodies in a way that makes us stronger and healthier, both mentally and physically. The way I see it, it makes no sense to essentially demonize working out as if it is taking some other aspect of your life away. Working out is a gift, and spending two months in the hospital bed will teach just about anyone that. Anytime I get a chance to move my body in a day, from something as mellow as a walk to doing an intense circuit training workout or weightlifting, I consider that to be a huge celebration. It's not something I'm just looking to get out of the way for purposes of staying in shape, vanity, or whatever one's motivation for working out may be.

My brother, Bennett also really helped open my eyes to a way of recovery that was completely outside of any knowledge I had received in the traditional sense. We did meditation work early in the mornings and breathing exercises that would increase blood flow throughout my whole body and into the brain. I would put myself into a trance of sorts and visualize positive energy traveling through my bloodstream and going to work on the damaged tissue in my brain. I would visualize my right cranial hemisphere (the region of my brain where the damage occurred) and the entire left side of my body lighting up with glowing blue light. The blue light I visualized was exactly like the blue light I witnessed when I felt I was crossing over once the brain surgery went south. I'm not sure what the blue light represents, but I know that it is good and that it was guiding me toward something great, so I figured if I could harness this blue light in my "mind's eye", perhaps it would improve the function of my left side. I was fortunate enough to discover early on the incredible benefits of using a pool to practice jumping in without the fear of falling. My brother would work with me on using my calf muscles and I would attempt to take steps and push off my left side on the pool floor in the shallow end. This boosted my confidence as the weightlessness of being in the water allowed me to mimic the many movements that the left side of my body once knew. I cannot stress the importance of pool therapy enough because the ability to recall movement with more ease in the water truly laid the blueprint for what was possible on land.

It was only a matter of time before the weightless resistance of moving my arms and body through the ambient water allowed my mind and body to know that I had something to work with. After combining pool therapy with breathwork and meditation, I would then attempt exercises in the backyard of my parent's home. I spent hours back there holding my cane, pushing my body and mind to new heights, all the while soaking in the richness of the sun. In these beginning phases, it was important to have my brother nearby as a spotter, just to make sure that I didn't compromise any progress that I made on a day-to-day basis. A bad fall or further injury was not part of my plan for success. I would never suggest that fellow stroke survivors attempt the liberties I took on land or in water without a spotter. It is very important to have someone with the strength to support you if and when needed.

Another thing I am forever grateful for is the environment I had been blessed to recover in. Especially after being trapped in a hospital for nearly two months, doing my exercises outside in the sunshine helped foster a major improvement in my mood and overall state of mind. I would practice walking barefoot across the uneven lawn with my cane for support and do everything in my power to keep my left arm in sync with my right leg, focusing intently on correcting the gait of my left leg.

Because of the aggressive tone (a side effect of stroke), this was no easy task. The tone in the arm and leg occurs when there is massive trauma to an area of the brain, which causes the arm and leg to coil inward toward the body. I was told that this tone occurs as a result of an evolutionary response to protecting your vitals from attack or further injury. Essentially, as it was explained to me, if you were to take a primitive human from tens of thousands of years ago and that human had sustained severe brain trauma, the brain had evolved to cause tone in the limbs of the body. This actually makes a lot of sense, knowing exactly what this tone feels like and what I would be capable of if I needed to perform such a task in a primitive state. So basically, if I were to put myself in the shoes of a caveman and I had this tone from my brain injury, I could grab and carry important belongings while I defended myself with my non-affected side. Seems like a ridiculous example, but that's how it was explained to me. It actually makes a ton of sense and adds up to a pretty logical reason behind the side effect of tone. Having prefaced this complex neurological side effect, the remedy to tone is simply to push against the natural reaction to coil inward. This is one of the most challenging aspects of recovery that I have fought against every moment of every day because it is a very strong involuntary reaction coming from a place that was outside of my control. Put simply, I had to learn to do the opposite of what my body was involuntarily doing. Fighting against this was by far the biggest challenge and took the better part of a decade to get under control. My vision is to streamline the process for readers going through this: understanding that doing the opposite of "tone" is precisely what is required to conquer "tone".

I kept up this exact routine and continued to make new advances toward my overall long-term recovery success for the better part of the year. It wasn't until about eight months after my accident that I decided to make a leap of faith and ditch my cane, mentally I was ready however, physically it wasn't quite an option yet.

At this point my girlfriend of four years had left me "for reasons unknown", and I was feeling self-conscious, alone, and quite frankly angry that I was still in the condition I was in. I blamed my disability and my poor physical condition for the failure of our relationship.

Unfortunately, there are major aspects of what I was going through that likely did cause her to walk away. I suppose it's better to see someone's true colors earlier on than later down the road. It baffles me to this day that there were such angels who stuck by my side and are still in my life to this day versus the people who could not handle my reality. Some people just cold-heartedly walked away or took advantage of me, while others rose up and lifted my spirits, day in and day out, and pushed me to keep fighting for my personal best.

With regard to the breakup, my broken heart spiraled me to a new low of depression and self-doubt, it was the last thing I needed on my plate. I didn't realize the ripple effect of what this breakup would ultimately lead to. For a time, I guess you could say I was a rebel without a cause because I felt like the worst things that could have ever happened to me had already taken place.

After a few months, I came to an epiphany and I realized several things that were hindering my growth. One of my realizations was that my cane was no longer serving me and I wanted to snap it over my knee. I couldn't stand being "the guy with the cane" any longer. I had finally had it. Although this was back in 2010, I remember this moment like it was yesterday. There is a big white awning covering the concrete patio of my parent's backyard, which extends from the back of the house out to the lawn. I was standing next to one of the pillars that meet the lawn, and without saying anything to anyone, I leaned my cane up against the pillar and walked away from it. The overwhelming feeling of accomplishment from this moment is something I will never forget. I get chills up and down my spine just thinking of this and reliving that day. An absolute monumental benchmark for my progress and a much-needed confidence boost. Remember how I was mentioning earlier, the unnecessary negative feedback I had received on what I was capable of? Well, this very moment set fire to all the negative rhetoric that could've held me back from breaking through this barrier. The neurologist who had told me, just months prior, I would never walk again without a walker, crutch or some type of cane was dead wrong. So this left me with a mindset of, "OK, what other barriers can I break through? What other statistics can I smash?" I walked away from my cane that day and never looked back. I'd had a love–hate relationship with that cane. Up until that point it had been there for me and allowed me to move around without a wheelchair and go places I ordinarily wouldn't have been able to go. However, I hated the reliance on my cane and the self-consciousness that came along with it. So needless to say, it wasn't that hard to say goodbye. Ditching the cane was the best decision I had ever made, but it also came with a ton of new therapy, realities, and training ahead.

Our normal gait is another major part of life most of us take for granted. In my case, the paralysis experience is unique in that it is 50% of my body yet 100% of my entire left side. Therefore, the right side of my body feels completely normal and functional, but the entire left side of my body feels tingly, numb, uncoordinated, and, put bluntly, paralyzed. Paralysis is no cakewalk and it takes an extreme amount of focus, dedication, and mental grit to make improvements through paralysis. Especially in the early phases, it really didn't feel like I could do anything at all with my left side, so to say training my left side and relearning how to walk "normally" felt awkward and clumsy is an understatement. But learning to walk again without the necessity of a walker or cane was truly the most liberating and freeing moment of my life. Being confined to a wheelchair for six months and only being able to walk with assistance plus the aid of a cane can take a major toll on anyone's state of mind and morale, so absolving myself from the reliance on a physical crutch gave me an indescribable sense of gratitude and independence. Because I was told this may never happen for me, it truly opened my eyes to the endless possibilities of reclaiming everything that was lost.

This was truly the beginning of me getting my life back and retrieving what had been taken from me.

Me skating pre TBI in 2008.

Snapshot of me jamming roughly 6 months before my accident.

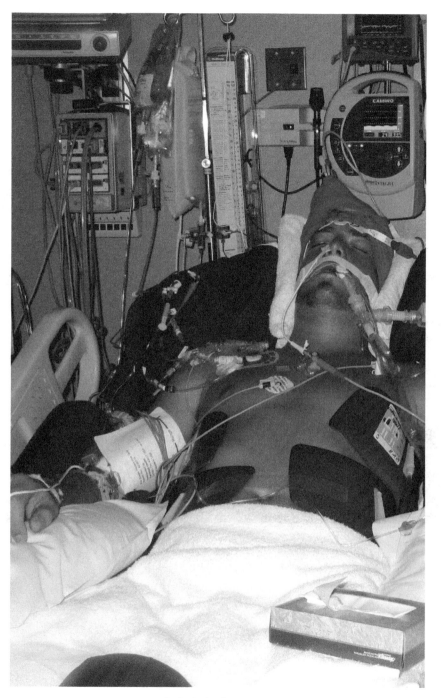

In the depths of a coma.

Hospital discharge day. I entered in at 205lbs and was released two months later at 150lbs.

2. A DECLARATION OF PERSEVERANCE

The greatest glory in living lies not in never falling, but in rising every time we fall.
- Martin Luther King Jr.

A s a quick preface to entering this section of the book, I feel it is necessary to touch upon a couple of things. Possibly the most valuable aspect of everything I have experienced comes from a place of ultimate truth. Living this has taken nothing but true grit and mental toughness; however, I am one who wears my heart on my sleeve, and while that can be good, it can also make you vulnerable. I quite literally have nothing but truth and honesty weaved throughout my experience.

The fact of the matter is that there is no way to fake getting to where I have gotten post-trauma. This isn't to say I have all the answers—because I most certainly do not—but it does validate the fact that I have navigated my way through trial and error, and successes and failures, so many times that I have had no choice but to learn how to grow from both the good and bad. The bad especially becomes our greatest teacher, which seems sort of like a sick joke, but I have learned to find truth and power even through the greatest of ego-smashing moments. The lesson is this: Be truthful, be honest, and not just with those around you but most importantly with yourself. As I said, you cannot fake it, you cannot pretend to reach personal goals or personal success by being a phony. Only the truth will guide you up off the plateaus that are created throughout the journey. Most of the plateaus I faced were a result of my own doing. I would lose my way, get distracted, and be less honest with myself and thus get stuck in a hole that I felt I couldn't get out of. However, as soon as I switched gears, I found my way back to truth and honesty. With the power of intention, I inevitably conquered every plateau, but it took an immense amount of perspective and time. Faking it and being a phony just simply is not an option for sustainability. Ultimately, you have to ask yourself some very difficult questions and the answers aren't always pretty.

Growing up in my family, my parents instilled values in me that are important for being a decent human being and a positive member of society. Do not lie, do not cheat, and treat others as you would like to be treated. That sort of thing. We were taught to be honest, forthright, and to also be brave. I was fortunate enough to have these values sewn into my conscience at a very young age, and when faced with adversity, maintaining these values was vital. In fact, I needed them more than ever before. I came up with the idea of a "Declaration of Perseverance" because I made a conscious effort to persevere through this obstacle and the many others that followed. I declared to myself that I would refuse to allow this situation to defeat me.

I essentially made a huge promise to myself that I refused to break. The promise I made myself was that I will never quit and I would relentlessly persevere through any obstacles that came my way from then on. I mean how much worse could it get? I had already been through one of the craziest and scariest life circumstances of anyone I knew, so if that did not break me, what possibly could?

Well, as it turns out, my problems were far from over. But the main point is, I created a mental declaration to persevere through anything life throws my way. That means maintaining truthfulness to yourself, keeping promises to yourself, and absolutely forcing yourself to do the things that you don't want to do because it is for the greater good. This greater good is not only you but everyone. I declared to conquer any life challenge and I branded it into my spirit. I destroyed the area of my brain that ever suggested I was incapable of anything. That was and still is my "Declaration of Perseverance".

Multiple Surgeries

I should also note that throughout this entire process, I was still in and out of the hospital undergoing rigorous testing to figure out any other possibilities that could have caused the initial stroke. I have been through just about every medical examination you can think of. Brain scans, cardiac scans,

MRIs, X-rays, multiple blood tests, multiple urine tests, multiple saliva tests, multiple reflex tests, you name it.

Transesophageal Echocardiogram

One of the more violating and traumatizing tests was the transesophageal echocardiogram. This is a procedure where a specialist essentially slides a hose down your throat with a camera attached to the end in order to capture images of the heart from within. I had already undergone several echocardiograms from the outside. However, in order to get an entire image of my heart, they had to approach it via the esophagus to capture the image from behind the heart.

The procedure goes as follows: First, mild anesthesia is administered to sedate me so that they could slide the camera down my throat without me gagging. A problem occurred. The initial dosage was simply not effective and I began retching, dry heaving, and biting down on the hose and they eventually had to stop the procedure. My throat was in agony and I felt completely violated. Unfortunately, because the anesthesiologist didn't administer enough meds, I had to come back for the procedure again. Luckily, this time they administered nearly twice the amount of medication to perform the procedure successfully. Once the camera was down the esophagus and positioned behind my heart, they injected my veins with an agitated saline solution, commonly known as the "Bubble Test". The purpose of this test is to see if any bubbles glide through the center of the heart. If so, this would be an indication of a hole in the heart. The way it was explained to me is that, as a baby's heart develops in the womb, there are normally several openings in the wall dividing the upper chambers of the heart, or the atria. These openings usually close during pregnancy or shortly after birth. If one of these openings does not close, a hole is left, and it is called an arterial septal defect.

I got through the procedure and then had to wait several nerve-racking hours to receive the final analysis. The cardiologist reported back to me that he believed that he saw two or maybe three bubbles pass through the center of my heart, which would indicate a hole but a very small one. He went on to explain that it was probably narrower than a sewing needle and that a clot passing through was extremely unlikely and in fact couldn't be the cause of my initial stroke symptoms. However, he did indicate that although extremely small, these holes can grow over time, becoming problematic with age. If I truly wanted to mitigate this tiny hole from being an issue in the future, the heart surgeon could close the hole through means of heart surgery. My knee-jerk reaction was "absolutely not". I had just undergone brain surgery that nearly killed me; I was nowhere near the mental state required to enter another operating room to undergo heart surgery. He went on to explain that this wasn't major open heart surgery but rather arthroscopic heart surgery, where they could enter the heart through my femoral vein. My position was still "absolutely not": My femoral vein was the pathway of my previous brain surgery, which came very close to ending my life. So, heart surgery via orthoscopic entry didn't exactly sound all that appealing either. The cardiologist completely understood my rejection and politely suggested I give it some thought and sent me home with an information booklet on the procedure, asking me to consider it after going through the booklet with my family. It was clear that this heart surgery was nowhere near the same level of risk as the brain surgery. However, it was heart surgery nonetheless, and although relatively minor there were still some inherent risks to the procedure. I had a lot to consider in this rather serious decision-making process. Part of me never wanted to undergo any medical procedure for the rest of my life, while the other part of me did not want to live in fear of receiving medical attention when necessary. Also, the fact that my cardiologist said it could be an issue down the road made me more inclined to take care of it while I was still young and healthy.

Here's the kicker: Anyone who has been through a life-threatening ordeal is somewhat weary of additional medical procedures. Having said that, if preventative measures can be taken to eradicate potential complications in the future then it is a decision that I'd consider strongly.

Heart Surgery

So here I am back in the hospital waiting to be wheeled into yet another operating room. As they are prepping me for surgery they give me some preliminary medication to help relieve any potential anxiety; valium, I believe. I remember specifically telling the room of doctors and nurses that I require more meds from the anesthesiologist than the average person so to please let the anesthesiologist be aware. They said, "OK," in an almost sarcastic tone, which aggravated me. I then said, "Seriously, whatever you would give the average person, double it." Do you think they took me seriously? Let's find out.

I woke up mid-heart surgery to the feeling of tools and catheters sliding around the inside of my heart. It literally felt like worms and bugs tugging and sliding through the inner arterial walls of my ticker. I opened my eyes, made eye contact with the surgeon, and said, "Uh, am I supposed to be awake right now?" Although slightly blurry, I have a vivid memory of this, followed by several doctors loudly saying in a panicked tone, "Holy sh*t, patient is awake! Patient is awake! Administer ***mg of **** now!" I quickly slid back under anesthesia and woke up a few hours later once the procedure was over.

So yeah, I woke up right in the middle of heart surgery. Never in a million years did I think I would be able to describe the feeling of having arthroscopic heart surgery, but here I am describing this surreal experience in detail. Luckily, everything went well as far as closing the pinhole in my heart and it is now something I should never have to worry about. This was a victory and gave me some valuable piece of mind, given my previous track record with less-than-favorable outcomes from surgery.

Intravascular Surgery (IVC Filter Removal)

I should also note that, while I was in a coma, doctors inserted an IVC filter (inferior vena cava filter) into my femoral vein for protective and preventive measures. The purpose of the IVC filter is to prevent and hopefully stop any blood clots from traveling through the lower part of the body and keep them from making their way into the lungs, heart, or brain while the patient is incapacitated for an extended period of time. The risk of vascular clotting is increased significantly when the body is in a state of immobility for an extended period of time. In my case, a removable, temporary IVC filter was placed in my femoral vein, which should only be in place for a month—a few months at most.

Not being aware of this IVC filter expiration date and removal protocol, nearly a year passed and the time to remove the filter was long overdue. The surgical access and procedure to remove the IVC filter is similar to the procedure used to place it. A small catheter-based wire loop known as a "Snare" was inserted into the large vein in my neck, aka the carotid artery. A removable IVC filter contains a small hook at one end and almost looks like an upside-down umbrella. With X-ray guidance, the doctor uses the snare to grasp the hook and withdraw the filter. Now, if a filter is left in place for too long, the tissue of the inner arterial wall begins to permanently attach to the filter, kind of like how a tree attaches its roots to soil.

We eventually contacted the hospital to inquire about when I should have my filter removed because we knew that timing was of the essence. Once the call was made, the brief conversation revealed very quickly that I should see a specialist ASAP to schedule the filter removal. Long story short, I went in for the procedure and they were unable to remove it because too much time had indeed gone by and arterial tissue was already attached to the filter. After a valiant effort, it turned out to be a failed attempt, and the surgeons explained that they did not possess the necessary technology at that particular hospital to remove the filter. Therefore I was referred to another hospital that did have the technology. The closest hospital that possessed the necessary equipment was Stanford Medical Center, which is roughly a nine-hour drive north of where I live. Let this be a friendly reminder that, as a patient, you also have to keep your best interests in mind and not let the grass grow under important deadlines. Technically speaking, this entire procedure and the complexity that was created were completely avoidable.

Before I go any further: This was yet another setback where I was sedated, put through an intravascular operation, and ended up waking up in the middle of the procedure. Just to reiterate, this now makes three very invasive procedures where I woke up in the middle of the surgery. Looking back, it was pretty intense to go through all the stressors and trauma of surgery only to find out that the attempt was unsuccessful and potentially dangerous. Because the tissue had physically grown onto the IVC filter, an attempt to pull it out could cause a lethal tear to the femoral vein.

My second intravascular surgery was now scheduled, and my dad and I road-tripped all the way up to Stanford Medical Center. Luckily, they had the technology to help me. Using a similar procedure, they entered a catheter into my carotid artery leading to the site of the filter. If you are unfamiliar with what a catheter is, think of it as a long, thin straw that can play many roles. In my case, this catheter allowed safe entry for surgical equipment to travel through my veins to reach particular sites that are otherwise difficult to get to.

In this new approach, Stanford Medical Center provided cutting-edge technology (no pun intended), where they could use a laser to cut away the tissue that had become attached to the filter. Normally this procedure would only take roughly 30 minutes, but because of the complexity of my situation, the procedure lasted nearly two hours. Believe it or not, this anesthesiologist also underestimated the amount of medication required to keep me sedated. I woke up mid-surgery for an almost comical fourth time! This time didn't just feel like worms crawling around in my heart, this one felt like getting stabbed in the abdomen. I woke up to the feeling of cutting, buzzing, and tugging on the inner walls of my femoral vein. It felt like a combination of sharp shooting pain while getting the wind knocked out of me. Again, I made eye contact with the surgeon and said, "Something doesn't feel right." An eruption of panic hit the OR and before I knew it I was back under anesthesia and woke up when the procedure was done.

Here is a little basic anatomy of the femoral vein. It is the largest vein in the human body and runs from the inner region of each thigh, where it ultimately becomes one in the lower abdominal region. From there, it disperses through the lungs, then through the heart, and eventually splits into the carotid arteries of the neck that lead directly into the brain. Coming full circle, these complex yet simple pathways were ironically the very arterial highways that were used in every procedure that I had undergone.

I am now in the post-op waiting room talking with my dad about how the procedure had gone. I explained that I woke up yet again in the middle of the procedure, which is a lot like a nightmare coming true. I filled my dad in as best I could, explaining the details of the stabbing pain of waking up mid-surgery and my confusion about how this kept happening. We chatted for a bit, sort of scratching our heads as to why I seem to be relatively resilient to the effects of anesthesia. When the doctor eventually came in for follow-up, I kind of threw my hands up like, "What is the deal with me waking up in the middle of surgeries?" I know this was not intentional, but this was the fourth time this had happened to me, so I asked, "How can I avoid this from happening in the future?" He sort of apologetically chuckled and said, "We all do our best, but sometimes things are just unpredictable. Evidently, God gave you an extremely efficient metabolism, so therefore the anesthetic drugs have a lesser effect on you. We have a legal limit and going beyond that limit could be fatal." He left the room. I wasn't angry, but my frustration was still there. However, what he had explained was a fair and logical response.

At this point, I was just elated to be done with surgery and happy that it was successful, despite the complications of waking up mid-operation. As odd as it may sound, this was just another step forward and positive reinforcement toward putting the pieces of my shattered puzzle back together.

3. ERA OF RECLAMATION

Capabilities, Not Disabilities

At this point in my story, I have covered a majority of the "clinical" aspects of my hospital experience. I apologize for moments where details seem foggy, but our brains have a defense mechanism, outside of being completely sedated. The mind will conveniently protect us by blocking out severe trauma in efforts to heal and move on. This is sort of a bittersweet symphony when it comes to processing what is necessary to overcome. Now, I'd like to bring things home on the "How".

When it comes to relearning some of life's most basic tasks and functions, nothing was more frustrating for me than losing the use of my left side, especially since I was left-side dominant. I had to relearn how to write legibly, eat, brush my teeth, and just about everything else you can imagine with my non-dominant right-side. I even taught myself how to use chopsticks with my right hand because of my love for sushi. Although I have gotten so much back and I am able to function very well, the fine motor skills necessary to write, type, eat, etc. were all severely compromised, to say the least.

As we are all well aware, using our non-dominant side to perform these tasks is no easy one; however, I had no choice.

The realization that I had to relearn everything I knew with my nondominant right side was a daunting, scary, and depressing reality check. Being forced into this realm of difficulty became the very backbone of my obsession with my capabilities, not disabilities. It served as the proverbial light at the end of the tunnel. I don't believe in allowing anything to hold me back; I only believe in focusing on the things to push me forward by having and maintaining faith in my abilities.

As you know, at the time of my accident my piano was everything to me. Writing songs was truly my everyday passion, and I was hoping to make a career writing movie scores for the entertainment industry. Since I was left-hand dominant, my style of writing was very bass note-driven. So, sitting in front of my piano for the first time after getting home from the hospital was pretty alarming to put it lightly. It was almost like being in The Twilight Zone; I could not maneuver my left hand the way I wanted to, nor could I even feel the keys underneath my fingers. I wished it was an old black-and-white episode of The Twilight Zone, but it was not and all I wanted to do was change the channel.

This broke me. I can't really put into words what that day felt like, I was in a completely new dimension of life. I came to the same realization when I picked up my guitar for the first time: I could not achieve one successful chord with my left hand. I can best explain this feeling as a twisted hybrid of sadness, uncertainty, and anger, and it was completely overwhelming. So much so that I turned my back to my instrument entirely, almost as if it had betrayed me, but I soon realized I was only betraying myself.

The good news was, my right hand was still 100% functional. After some time, I mustered up the courage to sit at my piano again and give it a chance using only my right hand. What I found was that I could still compose music with only one hand. This was a super frustrating process—much slower than I was used to—but it helped me begin to break through the mental barrier of feeling incapable. Of course, my abilities were not the same as they used to be, but I could still compose songs in a unique way and maintain my passion for the piano.

This delicate mindset of focusing on "capabilities" rather than "disabilities" was pivotal in my recovery. I did not realize it at the time, but this shift in focus was actually reprogramming my brain for the better. To dive just a little bit into the science of this, what was happening was a release of dopamine, a neuromodulator (the motivating driving force), and serotonin (the end reward) into my system—and, in a way, a complete redirecting of my habits and the mood associated with those habits. The release of dopamine motivated me to continue playing and it was the motivating driving force behind me to shuffle my way over to my piano and actually sit down to play. This, in turn, created a release of serotonin, a much-needed reward. Because of this awesome neurological process, I kept coming back to the piano and continued to jam and write songs to the best of my ability. As a beautiful byproduct of this process, I was pushed to set new and achievable goals regularly. As I regained skill and learned to become more capable as a right-hand dominant player, it got easier and easier. Even now, I continue to play music. I have even picked up the harmonica and played several live music shows since my accident. I get so much out of it, even though it's not the same as it was before in that I am only playing with 50% of my body. But it is completely worth it. This is just one example, but I have applied this principle in literally every other area of my life, and that is why I feel the need to share this with as many people as possible. The idea of focusing on what we are able to control versus what we are not able to control is no new concept. However, when faced with a major life challenge or when faced with any adversity, this seemingly "easier done than said" way of thinking, could never be more powerful and useful.

The lesson here is to focus on what you *can* do, rather than allowing your inabilities to dictate your mind and actions. To this day, I still maintain this mindset in everything I do, day in and day out. I can think of countless examples. For instance, on that monumental day, I leaned my cane up against the pillar in my backyard and walked away; my only focus was on maintaining my balance and taking steps forward. I put myself in a position where I had nothing to grab onto and no safety net because I was only paying attention to what I could control. My plan worked. It was a bit sloppy but successful nonetheless. It may not seem like much, but it was a life-changing decision, a scary decision, and that barrier of focusing on what I could not do had officially been broken down.

Multiple times throughout my recovery I have had what feels like an out-of-body experience. It's almost as though, as soon as I let go of the pain and suffering of thoughts that "I can't", there seemed to be a guiding hand that carried me through the obstacle. As I've worked to overcome the lingering side effects of my injury, I've derived power and motivation from harnessing everything that I was capable of, rather than dwelling on all of the things that were lost. If you practice this, what you're capable of starts to outweigh what you are incapable of. Celebrate and honor the wins, however small, and focus on what is there rather than what isn't. Soon you will be able to fill your day with activities that bring you pride, confidence, and a sense of accomplishment—and that is just the beginning. The sky is the limit.

Stroke Survivor, Not Stroke Victim

At about the year and a half mark in my recovery, I was only seeing my rehab physician roughly once a month for checkups. At one of my routine check-ups, my rehab doctor suggested I be a part of a research study at UCI Medical Center. Initially, I had zero interest, but then the more I thought about it, I realized that the reason I had no interest was that I was trying to bury my reality and I did not want to be a part of anything related to the word "stroke" at all. After all, I felt like I was on a good path and I didn't want to feel like a lab rat for some research study. However, after several conversations with my family and doctor, I began to gain interest. And, after all, what did I have to lose? So, I went ahead and signed up for the experiment. It was a four-week research study using robotic arm technology to see how quickly this may help with regaining mobility in a stroke victim's affected arm. I went through the entire study, where I met other stroke victims also involved in the study. You might be noticing how I'm using the phrase stroke victim now, as opposed to stroke survivor. The reason is, almost every day I was referred to as a stroke victim. Whether it was in the setting of the hospital, doctors visits, or in the setting of this research study, I was being referred to as a stroke victim rather incessantly.

For example: "Kevin, we would like you to meet another stroke victim." Or, "We have 10 other stroke victims in this research study just like you." "Kevin, as a stroke victim you need to blah-blah-blah." In fact, it happened to the point where I was referred to as a stroke victim anytime I was in the presence of any medical professional. I hated being referred to as a victim of any kind. It was a feeling I had kept inside for a while, purely because it was just commonplace to use that phrase. It wasn't anyone's fault for calling me a stroke victim, but for whatever reason, the semantics of that "victim" title infuriated me.

However, the problem with constantly referring to someone as a victim is that it causes negative effects on the brain. The more I was referred to as a stroke victim, the more it bothered me and the more I felt victimized. Eventually, after about the hundredth time of being referred to as a stroke victim, I'd had it and finally spoke up. I said, "Can we use different terminology for who I am or what I am?"

This particular therapist stepped back kind of stunned but also matter-of-fact, responding with, "Well you did have a stroke right?"

To which I responded, "I mean . . . I guess, but your phrasing isn't helping me at all. In fact, I feel that your phrasing is holding me back."

The physician apologized and made a conscious effort to avoid calling me a "stroke victim" for the rest of the research study. I wasn't being overly sensitive or anything like that, but I started to notice how constantly being called a "victim" was starting to wear me down—maybe I was even starting to believe it.

At the end of the study sometime in the year of 2011, my two favorite researchers invited me to speak at a premiere stroke awareness seminar that took place at the UCI Medical Center. If my memory serves me correctly, this particular stroke awareness seminar may have been the very first of its kind. By this point, I was feeling much more confident about my process of recovery, and after some thought, I figured doing a public speaking engagement might be good for me and help some others in the process.

As a quick side note, the concept of timelines does get a bit warped when dealing with severe trauma. I've had days that felt like weeks and weeks that felt like years. Having that said, I've also had years that felt like weeks and weeks that felt like days. Pardon the alliteration and slightly esoteric rant, but there is really no other way to explain this phenomenon. I no longer think of time in a linear fashion. I simply look at time as a commodity to use in whatever way it takes to improve my overall well-being.

Moving on... I accepted the offer to do the speech at UCI, and within a week or so, I was standing at a podium in front of a few hundred people. I had played live music shows before my accident, so I was no stranger to being in front of a crowd, but this was different. I didn't have my band with me, I didn't have my piano to stand behind; it was just me and me alone. They wanted me to share my story, how I was feeling about my recovery, and also give anecdotes about my experience with the robotics research study.

This particular robotics study focused on the mechanics and fine motor skills of the hand through the application of simple video games. For example, here's a funny visual. One of the video games that stands out in my memory to this day was a digital game where hot dogs were moving right to left on a conveyer belt and Homer Simpson was at the end consuming all the hot dogs. The objective was to time the application of mustard to the hot dogs without spilling it before they made it to Homer Simpson's mouth. There was a mechanism for my hand to squeeze, which simulated the action or dexterity required to squeeze an actual bottle. In this case, it was virtual. The levels would get progressively more advanced as the conveyer belt of hot dogs would increase in speed. This game was as frustrating as it was effective because I advanced to the final level and it supplied me with a sense of goal setting that ultimately led to a sense of victory.

Revisiting the speech about the robotics study, I definitely had some nerves because I didn't have anything prepared whatsoever, so I just "winged it". I figured the best thing to do was to speak from the heart. I walked up to the podium and looked out to an audience of staff members from UCI Medical Center, family, and friends of those who had experienced a stroke, and of course tons of stroke "victims" themselves. For some reason, the first thing that came to mind was my frustration with the phrase, "stroke victim". As I looked out to a sea of people at various stages of stroke recovery, I saw individuals in wheelchairs, with walkers and canes—and it all became so clear to me. I could see a version of myself in every attendee because I had lived through every stage of stroke recovery. I had indeed evolved from the coma ICU bed, to the standard hospital bed, to the wheelchair, to the walker, to the cane, and finally to my own two feet without any assistance. Each stage represented a graduation in the process of mobility and self-sufficiency. It was because of this very quick observation that I spontaneously led my speech with:

"First of all, I would like to say that there are no stroke victims here today . . . " A wave of silence cascaded through the crowd, and people looked at each other and back at me like . . . huh? I followed it up with, "But I do see several "stroke survivors!" This was followed by an eruption of applause.

I spoke through the applause and said, "Because I don't believe that any of us are victims here; we are survivors and that's how we have to view our lives moving forward in order to create the best possible outcome for our recovery."

The applause continued as I felt this incredible rush of euphoria like I had done something great for this community. I carried on through the speech, explaining my story, gave a shout-out to the robotic arm study I was in, and wrapped it up by explaining my philosophy of perseverance. It was one of the greatest feelings I had ever experienced.

After my speech, I had groups of people interested in talking to me. It was basically the same feeling I had after playing a live concert, which is an indescribable feeling of accomplishment and pride, but this was even better. It was also extremely humbling in this scenario, particularly because I had people in tears expressing to me how I had made their day and how they were going to approach their recovery with my words in mind. I was absolutely blown away and believe I coined the phrase "stroke survivor" that day. Ever since then, I've only heard the "survivor" phrase, as opposed to the previous and notorious "stroke victim". I don't know that for certain, but I definitely know I had never heard the term "stroke survivor" before that moment.

I got such a high from this incredible feeling of helping others and serving this community that I continue to speak at that event every year possible, along with other public speaking engagements at local schools and universities.

4. SEED OF STRENGTH

"Life is a storm, my young friend. You will bask in the sunlight one moment, be shattered on the rocks the next. What makes you a man, is what you do when that storm comes."
Edmond Dantès, The Count of Monte Cristo

The "Seed of Strength" is a metaphor from a mindset that I developed over a decade ago. One of my daily rituals toward the beginning of my recovery was to lie down on the grass in my backyard and record my thoughts with a voice recorder, like a daily journal. I would document where I was mentally, physically, and spiritually and note how I would utilize what I had learned thus far to continue to make progress. In one of my recordings, I was speaking about how I visualized tapping into my inner strength, and it goes like this: "I truly believe that everybody has the strength to overcome whatever obstacles life throws their way." I had somehow pinpointed the precise visualization required to recruit the feeling that leads to action.

Even though I was terrified of this unknown and new reality of mine, coming to terms with all the side effects of the stroke, I found what I like to call my seed of strength. The seed of strength may be lying dormant within you, but all you have to do is acknowledge its existence. That is step one.

Next, it's up to you to decide how to get that little seed to sprout, grow its roots, and eventually grow to be the biggest and strongest tree your mind can imagine. For anything to grow to this magnitude it requires ideal circumstances. For a seed to become a tree it requires fertile soil, sunlight, water, and an overall healthy environment. Similarly, a human being overcoming any adversity requires an unwavering drive to action, a coachable mindset, to give yourself permission to learn from failures... AND REPEAT.

I remember as I was recording this particular entry, I was lying under a huge pine tree. There were birds of all kinds chirping and singing in the background, which you can actually hear in the recording. I remember specifically having this epiphany of the seed of strength while looking up at this canopy that was home to so much thriving life. It seemed so fitting yet also ironic given the narrative of my recording at the time. The irony is that this huge pine tree I was observing overhead, like every other tree on earth, had started from just a tiny seed. I thought it was such an ironically hopeful and fitting comparison when it comes to people in recovery and what they are capable of doing with their recovery.

I had discovered my own seed of strength and realized that I was growing my own tree of recovery all along by watering and nurturing my injured brain. This whole experience completely changed my perspective on life as I knew it, so I decided to just embrace anything I realized that helped me.

This grew into a philosophy of mine, which is that everybody possesses their own seed of strength. It's up to you to find it and give it what it needs to benefit you in your growth to personal greatness.

Catch And Release

What I found multiple times throughout this entire recovery process is that tapping into inner strength most definitely is not always the easiest thing to do. Things will get in your way —the good, the bad, and the ugly. For me, when it came to things that were capable of slowing me down or bringing me down negatively, I had a bad habit of burying my sadness and sweeping my pain under the rug. At times this led to self-medicating which is not a good habit because it will sideline your rehabilitation process and burn valuable time.

The main purpose of this section is the concept that I eventually developed: *the catch and release.* The philosophy behind catch and release is that it is important to address challenges and setbacks head-on, while it is equally important to release these burdens that can be incredibly debilitating to our emotions and overall state of well-being. I've been guilty of catching some of life's burdens and hanging onto them, dwelling on them, or hiding from them as if they don't exist at all. The crazy part is that I didn't even realize I was self-sabotaging while it was happening. I suppose most of us are guilty of this disservice, but it definitely became a bad habit for me after my injury. The urge to emotionally bury anything and everything associated with discomfort became increasingly strong with each setback I faced.

One example of this was back in 2017. I had experienced yet another breakup that left me confused, devastated, and with a broken heart. I "caught" the negative emotions of the break-up, but I had a hard time "releasing" these feelings. I went down the slippery slope of feeling sorry for myself all over again, which led to further upset and some self-medicating with alcohol and bad decision-making. It really did start to get in the way of my personal and professional productivity. This went on for about a year, give or take and I felt that no one could possibly understand what I was going through because I didn't know of anyone else my age who had a stroke and lost everything. I was lost, struggling, and just got dumped by a girl I was assuming I had a future with.

It was sort of a slow burn that occurred over time. I would seek any distraction possible to try and numb the pain of everything I felt was lost. Everything from my broken heart, to my broken mind, to my broken left side, and uncertain destiny. It eventually got to a critical threshold where I began to feel like garbage all the time and it was clear I needed to make a lifestyle change. Not only did I feel like I wasn't progressing, but I actually began to feel like I was digressing. It became increasingly obvious that I had to take matters into my own hands and make a conscious effort to not only fix the issues I created for myself but also to reverse any further damage by taking my health and fitness regimen to new heights. It started to feel like I was teetering on the edge of a black hole that was trying to suck me down to my own self-inflicted demise.

Thankfully, I was lucky enough to recognize that this was getting me nowhere fast, that it made this burden even worse and it was making me feel even more distressed about it all. It all became so clear and the solution became quite obvious. The solution was to shift my attention from over partying, to taking ownership of my mistakes and leaning even harder into my nutrition and fitness. In turn, this became and still is my healthy obsession and I quickly realized that this is my way to "release".

Once again, this philosophy of catch and release truly applies to just about any obstacle life has thrown in my direction. By applying this concept to any hurdles that have come in my path, I recognize the issue, acknowledge it, own it, and insist on handling it with poise. It is essentially doing therapy work on your own mind and being realistic with yourself. You can only fib to yourself for so long before it starts to catch up with you, and for me, I became resentful and angry with myself. I began to not even recognize my own behavior by living a lifestyle that was untrue to myself and my deepest core values.

Catch it, own it, and release it, no matter how big or small the mistake or negative experience. It is important to execute this process in this order and in a timely manner to avoid a plateau and further wasted life hours. I eventually figured out that this catch-and-release concept is applicable and absolutely necessary in order to handle any number of life's burdens, especially when faced with an additional setback, such as a brain injury in my case.

To this day, whenever I encounter a heavy theme I remind myself of this powerful mindset. Catch it, process it, and release it. The acknowledgment of this philosophy has saved me time and time again over the past several years. I say this with absolute certainty: If you apply this process when needed in your own life, it will serve you just as well.

The Professor of Setbacks

You would think that my accident and everything that came along with it would be more than enough "setbacks" for one person to endure in a lifetime. However, the reality is that life can have an odd sense of humor and it can feel like we've been *Taken By Surprise*, more than just once. Since my accident, I have dealt with countless setbacks in life that probably sound hard to believe, but everything I have expressed and continued to share is nothing but pure honesty. I used to overanalyze every little obstacle in my path and try to determine the meaning behind it, but at a certain point it became too overwhelming and the challenges in my life added up to an immeasurable number.

I call myself the "Professor of Setbacks" because I can assure you that having a stroke is just scratching the surface of the loss that I experienced. Not only has recovery become a way of life, but the basic needs of life are an unrelenting constant and require every bit of your attention. If you don't prepare your soul for the ripple effect that comes from physical or mental trauma, then you will not be prepared for the next set of challenges when they come. Having a stroke can affect people differently, for example, for some it can challenge a marriage or relationship. For others it can compromise your ability to find work which can affect your livelihood. Your driving privileges can be revoked, and sometimes the people that are closest to you can really disappoint you. These aspects are just a small part of the ripple effect that I experienced. My driver's license was in fact suspended for over a year, it became extremely challenging to find and maintain meaningful income, and I experienced a revolving door of relationships with girls where I felt taken for granted, misunderstood, or both.

I am not sharing this with you to leave some dark cloud in the midst of a book that is about light and self-reclamation. I share this with you because these are all real life setbacks that I experienced and overcame myself. My hope is that by sharing this harsh truth with you, you won't have to experience the same obstacles, and if you do, then I hope you can streamline your approach and conquer your challenges in a fraction of the time it took me.

My message is to give love a chance, give life a chance, forgive people, and most of all, forgive yourself. Focus on the things you can control and work toward a recovery that brings you joy. Find a way to make money, use your mind and body daily, and set goals that are tangible and timely, but especially, be sure to apply the utmost effort on days when it seems impossible to do so. It was on the days I didn't want to get out of bed, or the days I didn't feel like pushing my body and mind, that I made some of the biggest strides in my recovery.

Those days quickly became my new standard and it is because of those days that I have found so much joy and, frankly, euphoria in the process of reclaiming my life. I strongly encourage this approach to anyone, for the sense of reward is truly indescribable.

Someone once told me to be "Bear Aware", which is an old adage of the wilderness and means to prepare yourself for the worst-case scenario. When camping in the wilderness it is crucial that you prepare your surroundings for the utmost safety from predators. Depending on the camping environment, you may have to suspend your food from a tree, padlock your cooler, keep a fire stoked, and be prepared for anything that might come your way. I've made this notion of being "Bear Aware" analogous to my recovery because it has been pivotal with respect to the overall process of anticipating what's around the corner. Put simply, do not allow the bear of your mind to sneak into your campground and take up the real estate of your mind. Most importantly, don't allow this predator to consume your comfort and free will. "If you're aware, you can prepare!"

Now that we are aware, it's in our best interest to be prepared for the ripple effect that is sure to come. As you may know, when you throw a pebble into a still pond, it creates an energy or a ripple effect that in turn is a play-by-play of life circumstances. When you see and anticipate the waves to come, you can prepare yourself no matter the storm. For every individual, the number or frequency of ripples may be different, but they are all relative to us individually. When trauma continues to rear its heavy head, it is important to remember that these turbulent waters will soon be still once more. Now that we have this ammunition and understanding, we are empowered to keep these still waters glassy and calm.

If I look back on my own personal ripple effect, I lost several weeks of sleep and my stress levels were at an all-time high because I allowed my reality to affect me way too deeply. I wasn't living in alignment with my core values and I was carelessly taking advantage of the fruits of my new freedom. It had taken me years since my stroke to earn the ability to function as a "normal" young man. I could effectively walk on my own, I had no cognitive deficit, I had earned my driving privileges back, I was a realtor, I was a personal trainer, and I was partying entirely too much in my free time. However, luckily for me, I have never broken the law and I positioned myself to navigate through all my transgressions without any serious legal recourse. I consider myself very fortunate and I now remind myself to never take that for granted.

This leads me to the notion of plateaus and how they are an absolute myth. Plateaus are weird and often disguised; they are wolves in sheep's clothing. Plateaus and setbacks are everywhere and none of us are invincible to them, especially when we are faced with adversity. These rather dangerous thought processes unfortunately become ever-present when you are in a weakened state, so it is super important to identify those demons in order to conquer them before they conquer YOU.

What I have practiced instead is looking at these setbacks as backhanded blessings as opposed to "bad karma" or punishment for something completely unknown and out of my control. I know and I have always known that my spirit is pure and I have never had anything but the best intentions for everyone around me, so why on earth would I be punished by God? So, I began to reevaluate how I looked at and felt about these multiple setbacks and life-shocking events. No matter how terrifying, depressing, or debilitating, I started to feel like maybe I was being prepared for something much greater than myself. I have done so much self-evaluation that I know every little inch of my psyche, soul, and personality. At one point, I'm not so sure that was the case. Not that I didn't know myself, but many times it takes extremely difficult circumstances to find out what we are truly made of. These circumstances can come in many forms and sometimes they are completely disguised. Mine just happens to be a laundry list of life-altering setbacks that you really cannot make up. I mean, since my accident, I have been faced with circumstances that have been very costly, not just emotionally but financially as well. I am not really at liberty to discuss certain details, but out of all the countless challenges I have faced, there are a few standouts that really held me back and greatly affected the course of my life.

One of the bigger ones was that I naively entrusted my financial well-being to a charlatan who almost single-handedly drained my bank account and completely destroyed my momentum. I had complete trust and faith in this individual, having no clue I was being lied to, deceived, and completely taken advantage of. Regrettably, I fell prey to this con artist who maliciously took advantage of me. Put bluntly, a lot of money was taken from me and I didn't realize it until it was too late. This obviously set me back, not only with my financial plan but also with my ability to finance my own professional endeavors.

Around the same time, completely unrelated, I was involved in a car accident, fortunately everyone was okay but nonetheless, it drastically stifled my progress and brought me stress I had never experienced and deep mental trauma.

All in all, this series of setbacks consumed seven years of my life during my twenties after my injury. It's how we handle ourselves in these moments that truly define who we are and the legacy we leave behind.

Each and every setback following my life's biggest setback, there has without a doubt been a silver lining and eventually a sincere understanding of the chaos. Even in the darkest of storms, we receive inevitable beams of light until the storm eventually clears. I have been left shaken up, sad, anxious, and angry, but with each tragedy there lies a growth of strength that is invaluable.

Each time I faced adversity, I reminded myself of the freeing liberation that I know is soon to follow. More frequently than not, it seems impossible to see the trees beyond the forest, but I've created a habit of checking in with myself to make sure I am not blinded by the thickness and uncertainty within the forest. It can be so easy to get lost and forget to mark your surroundings for reminders to get back to base camp. What I mean by that metaphorical statement is that it is extremely important to check in on ourselves and ask ourselves difficult questions throughout the journey of recovery. Too many times I have lost my way in the forest of life, and as a result, I have made decisions that did not serve me or those around me. I spent my entire 20s and early 30s as a stroke survivor with all of these countless setbacks from either bad decision-making or lack of direction. Watching all my peers go on with their lives with seemingly not a care in the world, while I had so much to bear. It could be extremely distracting at times and certainly sent me off course by not checking in on myself.

After my second bad breakup, there wasn't as much sadness or depression as one might think, or at least as I thought. I had a little bit of success and I ran wild as a nomad while burning the candle at both ends, yet again. As hard as it is to admit, I kept making the same mistakes and I wasn't being true to myself. There is no question I needed an outlet and I was pinballing through life with no true direction. I don't mean to beat a dead horse here, but it is important to understand that these things created more setbacks, and it was yet another painful reminder of things that I already knew. It was focusing on my fitness, nutrition, and sleep regimen that would become my new addictions and help set me on the right path: The path of least resistance.

Much like my stubbornness and refusal to allow my stroke to define me, I took those same principles and applied them to my goals of overall life success. Things that truly matter to me, like meeting the woman I want to spend the rest of my life with, and maintaining meaningful work that provides me with financial freedom but also a means to complete my mission of serving others who also face life-challenging adversity. I figured out quickly that these setbacks were capable of inspiring me to become the man I know I am capable of being.

That man lives by example and has the capability and capacity to help those that are afflicted and able-bodied.

Humility

Humility is an interesting one because, while it is extremely important to maintain a high level of self-confidence and faith in my abilities, it is equally as important to be humble. The definition of humility is: "Having or showing a modest or low estimate of one's own importance." As you can see, this is where the game of high self-confidence combined with humility becomes a very delicate balance. Too much of one or the other is not good, but when they work together in harmony, not only will it do wonders for your state of mind, but it will also help those around you who are trying to help you through this journey.

Because I've maintained a high level of humility, I have done everything in my power to avoid arrogance about what I've gone through and survived. While it may seem strange, it can be easy to slip into an arrogant attitude when overcoming an extreme lifestyle shift of any kind. Having survived a near-death experience is no exception. I think that sometimes it may come too easy as a defense mechanism, to point fingers and say, "You have absolutely no clue what it's like to be in my shoes." While aspects of this might be true, I have done everything in my power over the last decade to avoid weaponizing this truth because it serves no one. I have also humbly reminded myself that I am not the only person who has survived the suffering of a traumatic injury. There are countless cases of individuals who have suffered the consequences of a life-altering event. No matter how bad I have felt about the hand I was dealt, I acknowledged that I was not alone and that there are so many people who face massive challenges just like me, and some even worse.

As I had mentioned earlier, I have gotten to a level of recovery where I have successfully reclaimed most of my life and therefore many of the people closest to me may conveniently forget the suffering that I have gone through. I have trained myself mentally and physically to the point where it is no longer obvious that I have sustained massive brain trauma and what I went through might seem like a whisper of the past. I suppose I should take it as a compliment because Lord knows that my recovery has been nothing simplistic. To the naked eye, it may seem like I haven't experienced a fraction of the truth that I have shared about my life. Because my life is an open book and my recovery has truly been miraculous, I owe it to my readers to share my "Declaration of Perseverance". Essentially, it is a promise and a declaration to myself to persevere no matter what the cost. According to medical literature, I was considered disabled. I refused to allow this disability to "disable" my drive and spirit. I have developed an unwavering commitment to self-betterment and have become ruthless in my attempts to evolve as a man and as a survivor.

To reiterate, too much humility can make you too passive and vulnerable to plateaus in your recovery. Too much self-confidence can lead to arrogance and potential harm that will also make you vulnerable to plateaus in your recovery. The real secret here is maintaining a healthy balance of humility, self-confidence, and a declaration to persevere so that all of these states of mind work in harmony to your greatest benefit. While this seems simple on the surface, it is a daily practice of mindfulness and a meditation is necessary to get the best out of your recovery.

A glimpse of a carefree moment pre TBI.

5. FITNESS FOR THE INJURED

L ooking back to around the year 2010, I came up with the concept of "Fitness for the Injured", primarily because this was precisely what I was doing for myself in real-time.

Having grown up athletic, dealing with paralysis obviously slowed me down and had taken its toll on me mentally and physically, to say the least. I have had to relearn how to approach recreation, fitness, and exercise entirely. I have had to modify workout routines, use physical therapy tools, experiment with new methods, and basically do "whatever is clever" to achieve physical and mental progress. The psychological high that comes from gaining new abilities is a feeling like nothing else. Especially, when it's something you used to be able to do easily. Reclaiming an ability that was taken away by an injury can lead to endless possibilities. What I began to realize fairly quickly is that finding unique ways to approach fitness opened up not just one door but many doors to new abilities in me. The strengthening of my body and mind was creating and facilitating new confidence and motivation to keep going. Before I became dedicated to my new form of approaching fitness, it was almost like the curiosity and ambition I once knew so well had vanished forever. My new discovery of fitness for the injured unveiled those strong driving forces and allowed me to move forward in my life feeling strong, able, and confident.

I've always needed some sort of outlet or escape when it comes to the buildup of all the energy in my cells. Outside of music, it was either done through surfing, skateboarding, snowboarding, mountain biking, swimming laps, martial arts, or lifting weights. I played water polo and was on the swim team in high school, so I am no stranger to the water, but the idea of getting into a swimming pool with full left-side paralysis seemed a bit dangerous at first. However, getting into the pool for the first time was the most incredible sensation and one I will never forget. Of course, I had a spotter with me, Bennett, so I had the added security of not feeling like I was going to drown.

It was at this point that I realized how important and safe it was for me to get some exercise without the fear of further injury. As stated previously, it seemed intimidating to even dip my toe in the water, but it quickly became instinctual to just be in the water. It also provided me with the freedom of certain movements that were unachievable on land. For example, shortly after my acute rehab had run out, I needed to find a new way of doing this important work. Being in the pool allowed me to hop up and down with both feet off the floor of the pool and move my arms through the space of water. This mild resistance gave me the opportunity to rebuild my left-side atrophy by trying to mirror the capabilities of my right side. I would hop while moving my arms side to side, together and apart, building equal muscle tissue on both sides of my body. This was not only a huge victory for building up all the muscles that I had lost, but it was crucial in developing all the stabilizer muscles that are necessary for "normal-looking" motion.

For the next several months, we would go to the pool, and that was my energy outlet. I eventually got to the point where I could swim well enough to do a complete freestyle lap. Then I started experimenting with the breaststroke, the backstroke, and eventually the butterfly. Once I finally built up strength in swimming, I took my efforts to the gym to see what I could do. As an important reminder, prior to my stroke, I was an athletic 210 pounds. When I left the hospital, I was an atrophied and shriveled-up 150-pound dude at 6'3". Needless to say, I looked and felt like a skeleton.

I quickly found out that I could transition from the pool to weight training on the same day. I had a lot of work ahead of me and it was going to take months and even years of consistency to reclaim the body and mind I once knew. Going to the gym with my brothers as spotters allowed us to discover that there are some tremendous benefits to weight-assisted machines. For example, I could experiment with various movements, with different resistances, and there was no fear of dropping the weights or injuring myself. One of my favorite machines was the Gravitron, which simulated a pull-up movement by allowing me to stand on a platform and adjust the resistance as I pulled my body vertically upwards. This is where I realized I could do a pull-up for the first time in over a year and I found a new way to navigate my way through the gym. The gym became my sanctuary. Another fond training memory from early on took place in my backyard, where we had various dumbbells of different weight, among other exercise equipment. Closing my left hand around a weight felt nearly impossible at this point but I decided to start small by attempting to pick up the lightest dumbbell available, a puny 7lb weight. I realized quickly that holding onto a free weight, even a very light one is a much more demanding task than performing an assisted pull-up on the Gravitron machine. Not that the pull-up motion was necessarily easier, but the management of a single free weight in my left hand was just a different animal in terms of coordination. Surprisingly, after a few attempts I was able to pick up the weight for a couple moments, only to drop it directly onto the top of my foot while attempting to curl the weight. Deflated with this painful result, my brothers came up with an absurd yet successful solution. Spencer and Bennett had me grab onto the 7lb dumbbell again as they proceeded to Duct tape my left hand to the weight. This might sound ridiculous (because it sort of was) but it actually worked. It allowed me to retrain the active motion of curling a weight without the risk of dropping the weight or injury. Funny enough, this somewhat archaic approach not only helped retrain my arm and hand, but also my brain to keep ahold of the weight in order to perform the exercise. As they say, where there's a will - there's a way. It is because of that silly idea to use duct tape that I was able to progress to the point of not only increasing the weight I could lift, but also getting rid of the assistance of the tape. Once I had performed the exercise to the point where I felt strong enough, tape was no longer necessary to assist me.

Nutrition post-trauma has always been an interesting aspect of my recovery. Not only was there not a ton of literature on diet for stroke survivors, but I wanted to know what foods and supplements specifically would serve my brain and body health best. There are a couple of old sayings that have stood the test of time, and for good reason. "You are what you eat," is one, and there is another: "If you don't use it. You lose it." I took these notions very seriously and made a conscious practice of sourcing quality food, preparing food with extra care, avoiding harmful combinations of foods, and supplementing where it was difficult.

I find it bizarre to this day that I was in and out of doctors' offices for years and the discussion of proper nutrition never came up once. I've met with neurologists, cardiologists, intravascular specialists, hematologists, ophthalmologists, and general practitioners, just to name a few. One would think that diet would be a crucial element in treating any patient. I truly believe that for the stroke survivor community, proper nutrition, supplementation, and fitness are the pillars to conquering the side effects that accompany strokes and preventing further strokes from occurring. I strongly believe that this remains true for any individual. Personally, I had to make the subject of nutrition my number one priority because it was something I could control and I could tell it was benefiting me. As I jumped further into the science of specific food combinations and supplements it became apparent that this would ultimately become a life-long commitment.

It is beyond crucial to have a diet rich in protein and healthy fats and carbs to rebuild a brain and body in recovery. All the atrophy that occurs throughout the body from lack of movement cannot be restored without proper diet and exercise. I came to realize that my brain needed healthy fats like omega-3 fatty acids, choline, and the right balance of amino acids to not only improve my brain plasticity but also to regulate my hormone levels which then affect mood and motivation.

For over a decade, I have gathered from speaking with other stroke survivors that they were committed to a sedentary lifestyle and poor diet choices because they didn't know any better or they were afraid of failure. I feel that there is so much more education to be had in this department.

The reason I took my recovery so seriously is that it was all I had. Fitness for the injured is not only a concept but a way of life. My obsession with this concept is the number one reason I am where I am today. I say this humbly, but somehow I am more physically fit than most able-bodied people, so whatever I've been doing must be working to my benefit. This is not a statement out of vanity or a judgment of others, but it is simply a fact that my application of fitness for the injured has resulted in a healthy and strong recovery.

As I stated earlier in the book, I interchange between recovery and reclaiming and it is because of this that I have been able to reclaim so much of what was originally lost. My relentless pursuit has successfully broken down many of the grim statistics I was faced with regarding the side effects of a stroke. There's no room for an "I can't" mentality if you truly want to reclaim what was lost.

Balance

"Everything in moderation, including moderation."
Oscar Wilde

It should come as no surprise that balance has been the backbone of all these philosophies when it comes to recovery. You must have balance with physical therapy, balance with mental therapy, balance with nutrition, balance with work and life, and balance with entertainment and recreation. Time and time again, I had to drill these themes and concepts into my own mind in order to make them actually work to my advantage.

Maintaining the correct mindset and taking proper action on a daily basis is absolutely necessary to move forward. A healthy balancing act is vital to recovery, but it also contributes to avoiding burnout. Plateaus, burnout, and exhaustion are all phrases that are related to some degree, but they are merely terms for a place we never want to visit. They are capable of sneaking into our lives if we aren't careful to recognize them and defeat them before they defeat us.

From time to time, I needed a break from overanalyzing everything and being strictly "all work and no play". I had such a clear vision of where I wanted to go with my recovery, and everything I was doing was working, yet I found myself overwhelmed many times, mainly because I was not self-reflecting and celebrating my progress enough. I simply think of progress as a "nonnegotiable" and at times I didn't give myself credit where credit was due. I think what I realized was I was taking myself beyond my own personal limit and not recognizing my own capacity. It's important to work within your capacity, it is important to push yourself, and it is important to sit back and enjoy a well-deserved break.

After my accident, for a solid year, I didn't go out, didn't go on dates, or take part in any of the traditional "fun stuff" that a 21-year-old would normally enjoy. I did not even have my driver's license because it had been suspended after my accident. I am not saying that life revolves around partying and socializing, but a very normal aspect of human nature in our early 20s was taken away from me. Eventually, I had to accept the fact that I was no ordinary young man and that the freedoms that my friends shared were nothing more than a dream for me. I wasn't going to be traveling anytime soon, my school plans had been shattered, my heart was broken, and I couldn't enjoy any of the pastimes that used to seem second nature.

The fact of the matter is, though my attitude did not display it on the outside, my identity had vanished. Therefore, I had to find a way to break back into the rhythm of reclaiming my social life. I had to find a clever way to make a living and also stay on task with my recovery. This was the most confusing and intense juggling act you could imagine. Looking back, I still get a little sad thinking about all of the aspects of what it would've been like living as a carefree 21-year-old kid with not a worry in the world and my entire life ahead of me. That is an era of time I will never get back and one I will never forget. Sure there is sadness in retrospect because I'm acknowledging time I will never get back, but I was given an opportunity to gain perspective and wisdom that no one my age had experienced, and for this I am forever grateful. In a bizarre way, it was like I wound up obtaining an inevitable degree in traumatic brain injury recovery by having no choice but to live this life.

Circling back to my somewhat lonely 21-year-old self, the things that did keep me balanced outside of my support group were music, comedy, and the science channel. Those three things got me through some of the darkest hours of my life. Good music releases something inside of me that allows me to tap into my inner strength even deeper. There are a handful of bands I owe so much to, from the days of being bedridden in the hospital, to all the years of blood, sweat, and tears throughout my recovery process. I grew up being introduced to the classic rock scene by my dad, as he was a young man through the '60s and '70s and also played in bands growing up. But it wasn't long until I began showing interest in some of the heavier music genres and really became a fan. Therefore my taste in music has never really fallen into the mainstream genres that are popular among most people. I have always had a pull toward the punk, hardcore, and metal scenes, which also have a very cool and respected fanbase. I actually have a funny, vivid memory of lying in my hospital bed listening to Soilwork (my all-time favorite Swedish metal band), and a nurse walked in with an almost concerned look and proceeded to ask how I could possibly relax while listening to such heavy music. The nurse even suggested I try listening to some mellow reggae music or something calmer, but I explained that, while I sometimes like mellow music and plenty of other styles of music, this was not the time or place. I explained further by saying, "The reason I need to listen to heavy music right now is because it gives me the feeling of a massive energy release. It almost gives me the same release as training martial arts or getting an intense workout in or something like that." These heavy music genres have always spoken to me and these bands were speaking to me louder now than ever before. Creating the feeling of being powerful in a seemingly powerless state was an extremely uplifting feeling.

The feeling of being trapped in a hospital bed for months will make anyone feel extremely anxious and feel the need for a release. The fact of the matter is that listening to my favorite punk or metal bands made me feel stronger than I was. These are just simply the styles of music that get me going in high gear, but music is subjective to every individual, so I respect everyone who's passionate about the genre they love. I have unlocked areas of strength through music that I never knew existed. These areas of strength were unveiled at points where I was at the end of my rope, and I not only tied a knot, I climbed back up the rope for more. It really is an incredible superpower that music can give us. I have pushed through boundaries with the help of music that otherwise seemed impossible. There is something about it that makes me feel almost superhuman, the feeling of having your emotions stirred inspires motivation. Countless times I have felt the power of music and pushed just a little harder. I highly encourage this approach, especially when the going gets tougher than ever.

I have always enjoyed comedy, both standup and just good old funny movies. At many points throughout my recovery, during my lowest of lows, I would sit in front of the TV and watch a funny movie, even if I didn't feel like it, because what it did for me was invaluable, almost as invaluable as music, but in a completely different kind of way. Bar none, even at the points where I felt incapable of laughter or incapable of having my own mood lifted, at least one scene or one phrase would get me to crack a smile or even laugh a bit, and that was all I needed. It was almost like playing a round of golf, where you're playing terribly all day and you're not very happy about it, but you get that one perfect shot and it makes your day. Every other shot on the course that day doesn't matter, what matters is that one takeaway. I know this from first-hand experience. This idea of watching or listening to comedy was a trick I learned from Bennett. When he could tell I was having a rough go, he would suggest watching a funny movie; it didn't matter which funny movie necessarily, but usually one that would address shifting my mindset.

The power of laughter is a very underrated and under-researched tool, especially for people facing tragedy or adversity, and the best part is it's healthy and free! Sometimes I would sit and watch three or four movies back to back until all my worries and inhibitions were forgotten, at least for that moment. No matter what, I would come out of a movie in a better mood and often cured of whatever I had been feeling.

To this day, I like to start and finish my day with some sort of entertainment that helps balance my mood and inspires me to keep a balanced mindset.

Sense of Humor

Having a healthy sense of humor is really important during your recovery. There were countless moments when I wanted to cry, but I found laughter instead. Because, in a twisted way, it felt better. Being able to laugh at yourself is precisely what it takes to not feel sorry for yourself. I wholeheartedly believe that finding humor in pain can be an antidote to a downward spiral. I want to be clear, these are no laughing matters and I would never suggest being disingenuous with yourself. What I am suggesting is to sometimes take a pause, look at the situation for what it is, and find a chuckle rather than a tear.

This isn't the same sense of humor that I discussed earlier pertaining to standup comedy or funny movies, but rather having a sense of humor about your overall condition and recovery. At times, there were things that I simply just had to laugh about. I can't even tell you how many times I put my shirt on backward, had to retie my shoes, or I noticed my hand and arm has a mind of their own. Sometimes these things made me feel absolutely embarrassed and want to hide, but I grew to despise feeling sorry for myself and realized quickly the digression that is attached to it. The antidote is having a sense of humor about it all, laughing it off, and putting your shirt back on correctly.

I found that if I lacked humor in my situation, negative emotions would surface, build up, and cause me more harm. If I allowed this negative buildup to occur too often, not only would it put me into a mental slump, but it would last way longer than I wanted and rob me of any motivation I was hanging onto. The mind will play games on us, the mind seeks areas of comfort, and sometimes those seemingly comfortable zones are the most detrimental to our livelihood and progress.

Fear, playing the victim, wanting people to feel sorry for you, and being mentally soft, are all useless emotions and will put you in a dark place every time. Luckily, I never acted on any of these emotions because as soon as they crept into my mind and sat for too long, I would figure out a way to use my sense of humor to conquer them.

Even when I got dumped by my girlfriend just a few months after I got home from the hospital, I eventually found humor in that, believe it or not. Don't get me wrong, that was probably one of the biggest disappointments and for several months I was not OK. Feeling abandoned, unloved, and alone can plague anyone's mind, but there was an "aha moment" where I realized that my sense of humor would ultimately prevail and I discovered that I dodged a metaphorical bullet. I realized that there are plenty of fish in the sea and I was honestly grateful to be discovering this horrific news at that time rather than much further down the line. If she was willing to leave me then, she would have been willing to leave me at any other time.

The humor I found in all this was that it wasn't even close to the worst thing I had felt as a stroke survivor. Losing your ability to walk and write your name with the correct hand will play games with your mind, not to be believed. Having my heart smashed shortly thereafter felt like small potatoes in the big scheme of things. The loss of her still stung, but the more I reflected on everything, the more it oddly became humorous. Luckily, I found a way to smile at other things and move forward with my life.

Post TBI, fitness has become my number one priority.

10 sets of 10 pull-ups post TBI.

6. FALL IN LOVE WITH YOUR INJURY

"Don't think. Feel. It's like a finger pointing away to the moon.
Don't concentrate on the finger or you will miss all that
heavenly glory"
-Bruce Lee

Believe it or not, there is so much beauty sprinkled throughout the pathway of pain and tragedy, but unfortunately most of the time the beauty is not so easily seen. Beauty often camouflages itself in a jungle of uncertainty, fear, and anger. These philosophies and states of mind that I have either learned over several years or developed on my own are all interconnected to some degree. "Capabilities, Not Disabilities" led to my notion of being a "Stroke Survivor, Not Stroke Victim", which then led to the "Seed of Strength", which in turn led to "Catch and Release", and so on. Now we are arriving at "Fall in Love With Your

Injury". These concepts, including the ones I will continue to explain are all connected like a web. They are rooted in honesty, truth, bravery, and, more globally, looking out for one's own best interest.

This idea of falling in love with your injury was a relatively recent discovery. Not in the sense that I wasn't applying this concept all along, but rather this idea of falling in love with my left side was more of a subconscious decision. I realized that I had nurtured and fallen in love with my side effects when I was working out one day. I had so much faith in my left side to perform these exercises that at one point seemed completely impossible for me. I was going through my routine of a circuit workout that I had adopted from a friend of mine who learned it in his fire academy. The workout originally consisted of five pull-ups, 10 push-ups, and 15 air squats. This is all repeated 10 times. So, in doing the math, that ends up being a total of 50 pull-ups, 100 push-ups, and 150 air squats. These sets are repeated one after another without any breaks in between, at first this was extremely challenging for me, and quite honestly, I didn't think I would ever be able to do it at all. However, I liked the concept of this full-body exercise and the coordination it would require me to develop. Though my form needed lots of work, with every bit of my being, I managed to get through the first set, which was a huge milestone for me. I continued performing this workout daily and grew better and stronger, each time acquiring better form. Through utter faith and determination, eventually, I got to the point where I doubled the number of reps. This is where I truly realized that I had *fallen in love with my injury.*

At one point in my recovery, I would have told you that you were out of your mind if you expected me to complete this circuit workout, but I had faith in my left side, nurtured my injury, and flooded myself with encouragement to get the job done and evolve with the training. So much so that now I do 10 sets of 10 pull-ups, 20 push-ups, and 30 air squats just as a warm-up on my more intense training days. It is incredibly beneficial for both physical and mental strengthening and cardio. I am not trying to come off as braggadocios or trite, I am merely explaining this very powerful realization and what is possible. It occurred to me that nearly my whole recovery and reclamation revolved around loving my left side, believing in myself, and providing my mind with the necessary tools to have a successful outcome with my affected left-side paralysis.

Even within the medical community, I have been asked how I made this possible, and that is when it all clicked. I fell in love with my injury. It is no easy task but quite simple once I broke it down. I explained it like this: If you are to compare your injury with a relationship between two people, ask yourself what leads to a successful, thriving, and loving relationship. If the relationship is tempestuous, filled with negativity, judgment, anger, mistrust, or anything else you can think of when it comes to a toxic relationship, then the relationship will most likely fall apart, spiral into an inevitable crash and burn, and ultimately fail. However, if you maintain a relationship between one another that is filled with trust, love, faith, and encouragement, you give the relationship the tools it needs to thrive and grow into a loving, successful partnership. Simply put, by allowing ourselves to fall in love with our injury, we give ourselves the upper hand and a fighting chance for personal reclamation.

This same exact concept applies to how you view and handle yourself when tragedy strikes. Don't get me wrong, I didn't always have this loving relationship with my paralysis. There were times when I felt betrayed by my injury and the slew of side effects that came along for the ride. This feeling of betrayal turns quickly into anger and resentment and an overall depressed mindset. Fear, sadness, and resentment will, without a doubt, lead to the infamous plateau in growth or, even worse, the digression of reclaiming what was lost.

I know this is true because I experienced this firsthand and I have lost years of my life by doing things the wrong way. In my experience, the idea of falling in love with your injury is so powerful and so crucial that it is probably the number one piece of my broken puzzle that changed the landscape of my recovery and the reclaiming of my life. Just like in any relationship with another person, whether it be a romantic relationship, a friendship, or even a business partnership, what determines the success of all these relationships? Love, faith, and trust in the process. This is so simple it's almost frustrating to talk about because I wish I had realized this sooner. The beauty is that I was able to recognize this concept at all, and ever since I have never resented my left side and what has happened to me. Never will I take what I have for granted because falling in love with my injury has created a strength level that seems almost impossible to break. There are a few things I wish I had realized and applied sooner and the philosophy of "Fall in Love With Your Injury" is definitely up at the top of the list. I highly recommend adopting this mindset because it will not let you down.

The Power of Empathy

Empathy is defined as the ability to sense other people's emotions, coupled with the ability to imagine what someone else might be thinking or feeling. Having empathy has always been a very important way of living for me. The idea of empathy is so powerful because it allows us to not just care for someone but also to put ourselves in their shoes and see the world through their lens.

Being blessed with an amazing support group, I was on the receiving end of tremendous support from my family, friends, and community. Oddly, for several years after my accident, there were acquaintances who had somehow gathered false information that I had succumbed to my injuries and passed away in the hospital. From time to time, I would run into someone who would be flabbergasted that I was actually alive. Looking at the hope and excitement in their eyes that they had been misinformed is an indescribable feeling. Immediately the questions would start flowing and I have told my life story so many times that I figured this time I would put it on paper. The overwhelming reaction of excitement and curiosity of these individuals led to an incredible sense of empathy and understanding of my situation. Seeing and experiencing these genuine human emotions firsthand only crystallized my understanding of what empathy actually feels like and how I can apply this powerful virtue to others.

To be poised is defined as "having a composed and self-assured manner; marked by balance or equilibrium". In fact, I am so passionate about caring for others that I have started a movement called "Live P.O.I.S.E.D." (The Power of Inner Strength, Empathy, and Determination). The goal of this movement is to instill this philosophy into as many individuals as possible and provide a basic framework for those who are faced with adversity. A lot of this stemmed from the support group that I was so lucky to have, but I am aware that not everyone has the same level of support. This little reminder to "Live P.O.I.S.E.D" is to encourage people to never forget to tap into their inner strength, because without digging deep and finding a way you'll always be stuck in the same spot. If you don't have empathy, you will never forgive others or yourself and you will remain stuck. If you don't have the determination to do whatever it takes to improve your quality of life, nothing will improve.

For me, going through the experience of having a stroke, nearly dying on the operating table, and fighting for my life in a coma may suggest that I got a raw deal. But these events that put me in this position greatly affected my entire family and those closest to me as well. At times I even felt guilty, which I don't recommend, especially because these situations are completely out of our hands. But I couldn't help but feel terrible about what I had inadvertently put everyone else through. This is where I found the power of empathy and how important it is to be mindful of this way of living. It is a conscious effort and decision to be mindful of others and yourself.

Even though I was on the receiving end of this life-altering event, I had to maintain my understanding of what my family was experiencing by placing myself in their shoes. I really do not like the feeling of people waiting on me hand and foot, but when you are almost entirely immobile, that's, unfortunately, part of the equation. As I stated earlier, I have this bizarre feeling that I was possibly chosen out of all of my family members to fight this battle, but on the same token, they were put into the position to fight along with me. So, it was extremely important for me to maintain empathy for how hard it must've been for them to see me struggle and suffer through all the pain, trials, and tribulations.

As I've stated many times in this book, quitting was never an option for me. Fortunately, a ton of that came from within, but I also had the helping hands of my family to deter me from the notion of giving up. I would be remiss to say that the combination of the two was not working in harmony; I owe so much to my amazing support group. I didn't get to where I am today without a tremendous amount of help and it is largely my friends and family that have helped me arrive at the beautiful conclusions that I understand today.

Come to Your Own Rescue

I spent far too much time believing that something or someone was going to come along and save me from this undesired reality of mine. The truth is, despite being forever grateful for my support group, no one could come along and take this heavy burden from me. I had to work with it and work hard for it. It took me quite some time to figure out how to better my circumstances, perhaps way too much time. I essentially cherry-picked my favorite bits of advice, inspirational phrases, and philosophies and chose to live by them and honor them uniquely. "Come to Your Own Rescue" is a philosophy that is specifically tailored to anyone and everyone. It dawned on me that I had to become my own hero and in fact come to my own rescue out of desperation. This may sound easier said than done, but it really isn't.

For example, if you are swimming in the ocean on a powerful day with high surf, strong rip currents, and no lifeguard on duty, are you going to tread water and find a way back to shore safely? Or are you going to let the sea take your life? I don't mean to sound morbid, but there are some simple questions that need to be answered. To live or to die? To survive or to thrive?

I've spoken to way too many people who have thumbed their nose at inspirational figures, quotes, and philosophies, basically stating, "It's easy for them to say," or, "It's all such a cliché because they have everything going for them." My rebuttal to this is that it is equally a "cliché" and easy to sit back and point the finger and take zero action. Like that hasn't been done before. For inspiration and motivation to be effective, action is 100% required. Thus, coming to your own rescue is the only way.

Now, this idea of coming to my own rescue developed over time. I started to shift my way of thinking into ways that would only serve me. You do this by reflecting on how you would treat an infant, an innocent animal, or an elderly person in need. I asked myself, "Why am I so kind and compassionate towards others but I'm beating myself up for something that was out of my control and completely took me by surprise?" I started aiming the compassion that I have for others at myself.

No one could ever come to my rescue and create a means of income for me, fix all of my side effects, hand me a girlfriend, or come rescue me from anything for that matter. I came to the realization that this list of things I needed to change were things that I truly wanted and needed out of life and the list was seemingly endless. So, I had to come to my own rescue. I had to set goals, check in on my own progress, and celebrate minor victories. Over time, this would have a compound effect. Essentially, small victories would add up to large chunks of progress over time. Life inevitably throws us curveballs whether we are prepared for them or not. The notions of self-help and recovery that I have discovered over the last decade have come together into a symphony of unstoppable potential for me. I say this humbly, because I truly believe that anyone is capable of achieving this mindset.

Living a life day by day and taking mediocre action might satisfy some people. In some cases, there might be some very lucky individuals out there who have an extra helping hand, but ultimately it's up to us to create the rescue plan for ourselves. Coming to your own rescue means you have to be extremely intentional, not only with realistic goal setting but with your time and those you choose to spend time with. Time is our most valuable commodity; when you spend it you never get it back, so spend it wisely. This is your rescue plan. Always stick to the plan and always be prepared to adapt.

Coming to your own rescue does require work. I believe in working smart and working hard. I don't really believe there is one without the other. When we are working smart, we are using efficiency and putting ourselves into a position where we can actually win. It's not to say that hard work isn't efficient as well, but hard work alone will not get you there. There is a symbiosis that must exist between working smart and working hard with your recovery where "real" results happen.

It could be as simple as choosing to get excited about the day, knowing fully that your own heroic self is the one to fly in and rescue you. The rescue plan I created for myself began with my own mind, unlocking the cage that I had the keys to the entire time. By choosing to perform difficult tasks and electing myself to the hard grind of mental and physical fitness, coming to my own rescue became clearer and more achievable with each day. None of this was easy, but the more I held myself accountable, the more consistent I became in reaching the higher standards I set forth; therefore, coming to my own rescue simply became the byproduct. When it all clicked, it was almost comical. I found some humor in it funnily enough because this was only the beginning. Unlocking these limitations of my mind and coming to my own rescue created yet another snowball effect where things began to collect and connect. Once my mind was made up that I was my own hero, I began acting like one for myself and actually began to feel like one.

It really is crazy what the power of the mind is capable of once you figure out how to navigate it. I'll leave you with one last analogy, but is pretty accurate in my experience. Our minds can seem kind of like a dog that needs to be trained. It is a good idea to train the mind to avoid the dark and unsafe areas. You need to teach your mind to be silent, to sit, to pause, and to comprehend the performance/reward dynamic. While your heart and your gut will seldom sway you in the wrong direction, the mind will play tricks, it will bring doubt, fear, self-loathing, and confusion. So, it is best practice to train the mind to deflect these useless ways of thinking and feeling. Sooner rather than later the limitations of my body also began to improve and were rescued as well. Again, the ripple effect of these realizations began to take hold and became my new reality. I can honestly say that coming to my own rescue has been one of the most powerful tools in my recovery process and the most satisfying one as well.

I assure you with every fiber of my being, this concept will change your life. Come to your own rescue and don't be surprised if the greatest hero is the reflection you see in the mirror.

Bodysurfing post TBI has become a big part of my life.

Always finding an opportunity to celebrate my health.

7. MY LOVING MESSAGE TO ALL

Final Thoughts

T he side effects from my stroke and traumatic brain injury are still very much part of my reality in the sense that they lie dormant. And that's where I have decided to keep them. Dormant. They are no longer noticeable for the most part and I also choose to not be offended by them if they show up. As stated previously, it all starts in the mind. Then there is an unrelenting will that needs to be implemented in order to improve on all fronts. From there, it is necessary to take action and reclaim some of the simple life functions that were once taken for granted.

I don't say this lightly: Everything is therapy . . . and I mean EVERYTHING! Everything from getting dressed in a timely manner without assistance to navigating yourself through some of life's simplest actions is essentially the first ascent on this mountain that you are about to climb. I don't care if your first victory is simply putting on your socks using both hands. I don't care if it takes you 20 minutes to do so. Once you achieve this task, no one can take that victory away. Over time, the task of putting on your socks becomes easier, faster, and eventually mindless.

Much like playing piano, the independent workings of each hand dancing on the keys to create harmony is a multifaceted task. I have always used my relationship with playing instruments as a symbol of what it is like to function normally. When dealing with full left-side paralysis, there is so much going on every split second it can be exhausting, but once it becomes natural and fluid it becomes second nature.

I have trained my brain to control my left side at all times and it's only when I let my guard down that my side effects are capable of revealing themselves. The reason my recovery feels analogous to playing the piano is because I have dedicated myself to a melody of normal movement. I am always making music, I am always writing the symphony to my life. I move, therefore to the harmony of my reclamation is ever-present.

There is also another part of my brain that is taking care of my mindset and mood, which is paying attention to the rhythm of the other instruments in the symphony. Maintaining a steady mindset, not feeling sorry for myself, and not allowing my mind to waver and feel embarrassed in public were crucial for me to stay on tempo.

All of these things occur simultaneously as my right side is guiding everything else along almost like a conductor. This is simply my own unique musical reference for what it is to walk normally, talk normally, and function normally in society. There is so much going on every split second that it can be exhausting, but once it becomes natural and fluid it becomes mindless. Write the soundtrack that works best for you.

At the end of the day, I am a firm believer that we as individuals have much more control over the outcomes of our lives than we give ourselves credit for. For some people, it may come easier, but for many, it can feel like a long and grueling task. The constant questions we ask ourselves about what to do with their lives professionally, romantically, and creatively can be ambiguous, to say the least. For me, coming from a relatively artistic background, as a "feeler" or a "creative soul", my ambition has been unique and certainly has never truly aligned with pursuing a life in the traditional sense.

I have always had a strong magnetic pull toward doing things in a very "outside of the box" manner. It didn't matter if it was learning new material in school, figuring out how to play a new instrument, or learning a new skateboard trick, I have always done things in my own unique way. This is not to say that I object to people's suggestions when it comes to learning a new craft; however, I have just figured out a way to have enormous faith in my abilities. I never realized how much this would serve me until I was faced with a situation that at times felt like a complete nightmare that I could never wake up from.

The whole reason I decided to write this book was that I would be completely remiss not to share my story of perseverance in hope that it will save people from themselves and the grip of pain that life is capable of holding. Everything since the very beginning has been nothing short of a challenge, as we all face challenges in this life. The problem is, there are very few legitimate remedies to these challenges, and the bigger the challenge, the more difficult the remedy is to find. That is why I ultimately decided to put ink to paper regarding my life experience and help those that are lost.

As I have stated before, I wish I had my future self to confide in when I was in my darkest hours. I had no idea the challenge I was up against and there was no one there to guide me who had experience in this field. Doctors and nurses do an incredible job keeping us glued together when we need help in a clinical sense. The answers to the issues I was facing were not relatable to the people that were trying to help me the most. I found clarity on where I was heading through my own experience. I don't know if it was dumb luck, an iron will to overcome, or a combination of the two, but somehow everything collided beautifully.

I essentially had to create my new identity while maintaining a strong sense of who I am and where I come from, and never forgetting my pre-existing core values. This isn't to say we shouldn't change, as I believe changing ourselves and creating an identity that serves us is at the very center of true recovery and reclaiming our lives post-trauma. My previous identity revolved around music, action sports, and my girlfriend, but as soon as all of that was taken away, it became increasingly difficult to understand myself, what to do with my life, or where I was headed.

I am here today in the flesh as a result of good decisions that just happened to outweigh the bad ones. The last thing I want to see is my fellow brothers and sisters go through unnecessary suffering as I did. The only reason that I suffered was that I lost sight of my dreams to be my best self.

Learning and understanding how to maintain the proper mindset when all odds are stacked against you is no picnic, and I am here as proof that there is a recipe for success after all. And it happens to be way easier done than said.

In this book, I have shared my life story. I have shared my "Declaration of Perseverance", where I have declared that this harsh reality is not my identity. I have shared my "Era of Reclamation", which includes "Capabilities, Not Disabilities" and "Stroke Survivor, Not Stroke Victim". When we focus on capabilities rather than disabilities we are doing ourselves a favor by focusing on what is possible rather than what you believe is impossible. When we change our self-speech from stroke victim to stroke survivor, we not only survive, we thrive.

I have shared the power of mindset through having the smallest "Seed of Strength". From that spawns the blueprint for living P.O.I.S.E.D., which stands for the "Power of Inner Strength, Empathy, and Determination". My overall vision for "Fitness for the Injured" is simply the application of the "how" to strengthen the mind, body, and spirit. "Fall in Love With Your Injury", is the right of passage and final acceptance of inner peace.

My loving message to all is to live with beautiful intention and live P.O.I.S.E.D.

ABOUT THE AUTHOR

Kevin Gocke grew up as an avid board sportsman, martial arts enthusiast, and musician, who was suddenly "taken by surprise" just two years out of high school. He was forced into an unexpected situation where he had to make some serious life decisions at a very young age. Waking up from a coma with full left-side paralysis and left-side blindness, and having spent his 21st birthday unconsciously fighting for his life, he would embark on a journey to regain the life he once knew in a powerful way. He refers to this phenomenon as his "Declaration of Perseverance". Because Kevin feels these practices are so profound, he has dedicated his life to perfecting the art of living as a survivor rather than a victim. As a result of his passion for rebuilding the wreckage of his former life, Kevin has created quite a positive and successful life regardless of the countless setbacks that have tried to stifle his personal growth and life progress. Despite these challenges, Kevin has become a health and fitness advocate, a certified personal trainer, a successful realtor, published author, and in the year 2022 Kevin entered into a loving marriage with his wife Kayla. His true passion has become sharing his deep experience and knowledge of stroke recovery by serving those who are held back by the limitations of their own mind, body, and spirit by proving what is possible.

TAKEN BY SURPRISE

Made in the USA
Monee, IL
16 March 2025

14055491R00079